THE
FIRST
MINUTES

What to Do Until the Ambulance Arrives
Revised Edition

Alexander M. Butman, EMSI, REMT-P
Edward L. Pendagast, Jr., MD

To those members of the public who have taken the time to learn what to do, and who in a sudden emergency render aid to their fellow man.

The authors wish to express their thanks to Judith H. Demarest, Susan L. Brown and Steven E. Reinberg for their assistance in the writing and editing, and again to Susan for the photography of the original 1984 edition. We also wish to thank Edward A. Casker for the cover and text design.

For the Revised Edition, a special thanks to Tom Petrich who did the graphics and to Vincent A. Greco for the new photography. Our thanks also to Jeannie Montgomery and Rick Vomacka who assisted in determining the necessary changes and in editing the revised manuscript.

Rapid Reference Pages:

Contents

Chapter 1
The First Minutes

What would you do if your child started to choke? Or if you discovered a coworker unconscious and not breathing? What would you do if you stopped at an automobile accident and found a victim bleeding severely? You'd probably send for an ambulance. But what then? What do you do while you wait for help to arrive?

This book is designed to answer that question. It is not a general medical guide, but a specific summary of those measures you can take during the first minutes of a life-threatening emergency—while help is on the way.

This book is different from other first-aid books in that it concentrates only on those first crucial minutes. It assumes that professional help is no more than 10–20 minutes away—the average response time for ambulances.

Every condition described in this book is a true emergency. Each condition requires an ambulance and treatment in a hospital emergency department. Nothing should delay you in calling for an ambulance. Your treatment is not a substitute for prompt professional aid. However, what you do after you call for help can mean the difference between life and death.

The techniques and skills presented here are simple and easy to learn—and you won't need any equipment. But they do need to be reviewed and practiced. And the time to learn these skills is *now,* not when the emergency occurs.

One technique, CPR (cardiopulmonary resuscitation), cannot be learned solely from a book. It is a skill that must be practiced on a CPR manikin. Both the American National Red Cross and the American Heart Association offer CPR courses regularly. Contact your local chapter for details.

If you are a camper, a hiker, a cross-country skier, a mountaineer—someone who spends time in remote, hazardous places—you should consider training beyond what is contained here. The American National Red Cross course in advanced first aid is available from you local Red Cross. Your local ambulance service may also offer emergency training classes. Such courses require time and effort, but if you intend to be out of reach of medical aid, you would be wise to take advantage of them.

But most of the time, the ambulance is close by, and in most communities, ambulances are staffed by emergency medical technicians—EMTs. These EMTs—either paid or volunteer—are on call to help. They are backed by emergency physicians, nurses, and other professional hospital staff, all dedicated to saving lives. They are part of a prehospital-care system that helps assure you of uniform emergency care wherever you are. But the system only works with your involvement. Your ability to aid a victim during those critical first minutes, and to swiftly mobilize the Emergency Medical Service system, will help save lives.

What Is an Emergency?

When a medical emergency occurs, generally you will know it. You can tell by the seriousness of the situation, or by the type of injuries you see, or by the way the patient looks, that it's time to call an ambulance. You should call an ambulance whenever the situation is more than you can handle. Here is a list of some instances when calling an ambulance is definitely the right thing to do:

- Any accident with injuries
- Major bleeding
- Drowning
- Electric shock
- Possible heart attack
- Difficulty breathing
- Choking (Obstructed Airway)
- Absence of breathing
- Unconsciousness
- Poisoning
- Attempted suicide
- Sudden violent illness, seizures or convulsions
- A severe episode of a known condition
- Serious burns
- Severe abdominal pain
- Paralysis
- Imminent childbirth

When situations this serious occur, do not call your doctor, the hospital, a friend, relatives, or neighbors for help. Call the *Ambulance.* Calling anyone else will only waste time and put the patient in greater jeopardy.

Over the past years, each community has developed an EMS system. EMS stands for Emergency Medical Services. Today the Emergency Ambulance will respond to you staffed by State Certified Emergency Medical Technicians (EMT's). When you have an acute medical emergency you should call your local Emergency Medical Services (EMS) number for assistance and an Emergency Ambulance.

Calling the ambulance has several important advantages.

1. Many patients should not be moved except by trained personnel.
2. The EMTs that arrive with the ambulance know what to do. In addition, they are in radio contact with physicians at the hospital.
3. Care provided by EMTs at the scene and on the way to the hospital will have a meaningful impact on a patient's chances of survival and rate of recovery.
4. Time will be saved in getting the patient to the hospital.

If the situation is not an emergency, call your doctor. However, if you are in any doubt as to whether the situation is an emergency, call EMS for the ambulance.

How to Call for an Ambulance

Just as important as knowing when to call for help is knowing *how* to call. Giving the right information in the right order will bring help faster.

Be sure that you know the emergency number in your area. In most communities the police, fire, and ambulance services use the same number. If you don't know your local emergency number, look on the first page of your telephone book. Many areas use 911 for all emergencies. Other areas use a different system. Whatever the number is, you should post it by each phone in your house and write it in the front of all of your phone directories.

In most cases, when you call for emergency help, the person you speak to is a *dispatcher.* It is the dispatcher's job to gather information from you and send the ambulance or other help. The dispatcher may or may not know emergency medical procedure, so do not expect specific instructions in first aid. Instead, simply give the information needed to get the ambulance rolling. After that, the dispatcher may be able to give some instructions. Keep your voice calm and speak clearly so the dispatcher can understand you. If you have to repeat yourself, you are wasting precious time. Give the dispatcher the following information, in this order:

1. Your name.
2. The telephone number you are calling from. (The dispatcher needs this information in case you are disconnected. Knowing your number, the dispatcher can call you back or find you by the location of the telephone.)
3. The *complete* address or location where the patient can be found. Name the town. Many adjacent communities served by the same EMS system have duplicate street names. (Include the apartment number if there is one.)

4. The nature of the problem (e.g., car accident) and the condition of the patient (e.g.,
unconscious or bleeding severely). This will
help the dispatcher decide what help to
send. The dispatcher may ask the patient's
age, whether he or she is unconscious, and
whether he or she is breathing normally.
All of this information can help the EMTs
prepare for the emergency you are expe-
riencing.
5. *Do not hang up.* The dispatcher may need
additional information or have instructions
for you. Let the dispatcher end the conver-
sation.

In addition it may be helpful to give the dispatcher the nearest cross street or major landmark.
For car accidents, the number of the nearest utility
pole or the address of the nearest house will be helpful. On limited-access highways (freeways, toll roads),
you can give the number of the nearest exit, and the
direction of travel. Giving good directions is very important. It saves time and lives.

In a situation such as a car accident, where it is
necessary to travel to find help, you should stay with
the patient, if possible, in order to give aid. If you
must rely on passersby to go for help, send at least
two. This should ensure that help *will* be called. Don't
rely on a single person, who may promise to call for
help but fail to do so.

Of course, if you have a CB radio, or if a car
stops that has one, this is an excellent way to get
help, as most police monitor channel 9, the emergency channel. Give the same information you would
give to a dispatcher, remembering to speak clearly.

In situations where you feel the ambulance will find it hard to locate you, have someone wait at a visible spot to guide the ambulance when it arrives.

In all cases, after you have called for help, you should remain with the patient and render whatever aid you can. After the ambulance has been called is the time to notify the patient's doctor, if there is one. If the patient is currently taking any medicines, be sure that these are ready to be taken with the patient to the hospital.

Don't Become a Victim

Don't unnecessarily risk your life to save another. There are many situations that require special training to effect a rescue. If you are not a strong swimmer, don't jump into the water after a drowning person. If you are not trained in mountain rescue, don't attempt to go to someone trapped on a ledge. Don't become a victim. Do not attempt any rescue that is beyond your capability. EMTs and rescue crews are specially trained and equipped to handle hazardous situations safely. Leave the rescue to them.

When the ambulance arrives, the EMTs will want to go right to the patient. They will then examine the patient and take the vital signs (respirations, pulse, blood pressure, etc.). They will ask both you and the patient a variety of questions about what happened. They will also ask the patient's medical history. Whenever possible, you should let the patient answer these questions. EMTs are concerned not only with the answers, but with *how* the patient answers. It may appear that they are wasting time and going too slowly. Don't be alarmed: they need the information and the results of their exam to treat the patient.

Finding Out What's Wrong

Most people who die in the first minutes after an accident or medical emergency die because of the body's inability to maintain adequate circulation and ventilation. The problem may be a heart attack, choking, an allergic reaction, or any of a number of illnesses—but the specific, immediate cause of death is that the vital organs were not getting enough oxygen. That's why it is your job in those first minutes to evaluate whether circulation and ventilation are adequate, and if they are not, to support those body functions until help arrives. Even if the victim appears to be all right, it is up to you to watch the victim for any sign of trouble or change in condition, so that you can give the necessary help. You must know *what* to do and *when* to do it.

What follows is a guideline: a quick way to look at a victim and analyze a situation to determine if an emergency is occurring—and what needs to be done. Try to approach all victims this way, regardless of the apparent cause of the problem.

1. Is the scene safe?
2. Is the victim breathing normally?
3. Is the victim bleeding? Are there any apparent injuries?
4. Is the victim conscious and alert, or unconscious?
5. What happened?
6. Should the victim be moved?

1. Is the scene safe? The first thing you should determine is whether the scene is safe for you to enter. If there is fire, an electrical hazard, or toxic fumes, it is best to stay away. Summon help and prevent others from entering the scene until professional help arrives. Don't become the next victim!

2. Is the victim breathing normally? If the victim is breathing normally, you know that he or she is probably getting enough oxygen to maintain life. Normal breathing is effortless and quiet, and you can see and feel the rising of the chest with each breath. Abnormal breathing may be characterized as either too rapid, too slow, too noisy, or too difficult. Abnormal breathing is often noisy—gasping, wheezing, etc., or the patient is obviously working very hard to get air. Any abnormal breathing tells you that an emergency exists.

If the victim is not breathing normally or not breathing at all, you may have to assist ventilation with mouth-to-mouth resuscitation or provide cardiopulmonary resuscitation—CPR. You will have to move the head to open the airway. So when you evaluate breathing, you should decide if a spine injury is likely. If it is, you will have to be very careful how you move the victim's head and neck. The quickest way to make this judgment is to ask yourself if this type of accident *could* have injured the patient's head, neck, or back. If the answer is yes, assume that spine injury *is* present and be sure not to move the patient unless absolutely necessary. If CPR must be given, however, the patient will have to be moved into the cardiac arrest position (flat on the back on a hard surface) regardless of the injuries.

Because breathing is so important you should

monitor every patient's breathing even if it appears normal. In addition, should the patient vomit you must be sure that the airway remains clear and open.

3. Is the victim bleeding? Are there any apparent injuries? If you see obvious major bleeding, you must attempt to stop it at once and treat for shock. (You should also note any signs of obvious injury, such as broken bones.) You can learn a good deal about the patient's condition from the *quality* of the pulse. It is not necessary for you to take the pulse rate; you do not have to count the beats. Instead, *feel* the pulse to see if it is reasonably strong and regular; this means circulation is good. However, if it is weak or very fast or irregular, the patient is having a circulatory problem.

To feel the pulse, place the tips of your three long fingers on the thumb side of the patient's wrist, just at the side of the bone. Press gently. You should feel a pulse called the *radial* pulse. Practice this on yourself until you can find the radial pulse easily. You can use this pulse with most patients.

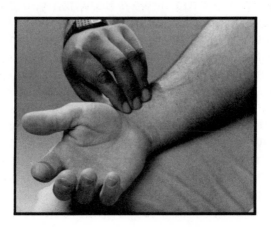

You should also observe *skin color.* If the patient is blue, or pale or ashen, there may be circulatory problems. If the patient looks bluish on the lips or under the fingernails—a condition called cyanosis—this is a sign of serious circulatory or respiratory malfunction. The organs are not receiving enough oxygen. The patient needs immediate medical attention.

4. Is the victim conscious and alert, or unconscious? If the victim is conscious and alert, this is a sign that the condition is fairly stable. If the victim is conscious but disoriented or slow to respond to your voice or touch, this is a sign that the condition may be serious. If the victim is unconscious, help is needed immediately.

5. What happened? Learning what happened can give you a clue as to what injuries or problems are likely. When possible, the victim should be allowed to give this information. The way the victim talks can be a good indicator. If speech and memory are normal, this is a good sign. If you detect problems in speech or memory, or if the victim goes in and out of consciousness or has any problems giving a coherent report, you can be fairly sure that the situation is serious. You should find out if the patient is suffering from any existing medical problems or taking any medications or if he or she is allergic to any medicine or food. If the victim is unconscious you should look for a bracelet or necklace (Medi-Alert) that indicates an existing Medical condition. (The victim should be allowed to give the same report to the EMTs when they arrive.) Also remember, you can learn a lot by simply looking at the patient. You can tell when something is seriously wrong by the way the patient looks, speaks, or moves. You can trust your instinct: if the patient looks bad, generally the condition is serious.

6. Should the patient be moved? Is there any hazard requiring that the patient be moved? If not, the patient should be treated where he or she is. The patient should only be moved by trained EMS personnel.

What to Do First

Regardless of the nature of the accident or medical problem, you should try to handle the situation as follows:

- Determine if the scene is safe.
- Determine the victim's condition:
    1. Breathing?
    2. Bleeding?
    3. Conscious?
    4. What happened?
- Call for an ambulance (or be sure someone else has called). Remember, nothing you do should delay the summoning of professional help.
- Begin treatment. Always treat the most severe (life-threatening) problems first. Generally, follow this order:
    1. Airway
    2. Respiratory Arrest or Cardiac Arrest (both respiratory and Cardiac Arrest).
    3. Major bleeding
    4. Most severe wound
    5. Shock
    6. Other

A good way to remember the key part of the sequence is to follow the alphabetical order. That is, to treat the A,B,C,'s.

A—Airway
B—Breathing
C—Circulation, (Severe bleeding or Cardiac Arrest).

Chapter 2
Basic Life Support

Every cell in the body needs oxygen to live. When we breath, air containing oxygen is taken in and a good oxygen level is maintained in the lungs. From the lungs, oxygen passes into the blood stream. The heart's beating pumps the blood around the Circulatory System. This circulates oxygen to the parts of the body—where it passes out of some blood vessels (capillaries) and into the cells. Proper ventilation (breathing) *and* circulation are needed to provide oxygen. Without oxygen for more than six minutes, irreversible cell death starts occurring in the brain and other vital organs. When cells start dying, "biological death" has commenced.

When the patient is in full cardiac arrest he will have neither breathing or circulation, and is said to be "clinically dead". Victims in cardiac arrest need Cardiopulmonary Rescusitation—CPR. CPR combines artificial ventilation with artificial circulation. This combination provides oxygen to the lungs and circulation to get the oxygen to the brain and other body cells. The aim of the timely institution of CPR is to prevent *clinical death* from becoming irreversible *"biological death."*

Basic Life Support is providing the essential vital needs that the patient can no longer provide for himself. If he can not keep his airway clear—the rescuer opens the airway. If he is not breathing, but still has circulation—the rescuer provides artificial ventilation.

If he is in full cardiac arrest—the rescuer provides an airway, ventilation, and circulation by doing CPR.

Respiratory Arrest

Respiratory arrest means that breathing has stopped. The cause can be medical (illness) or trauma (injury). It is possible for breathing to stop while the heart continues to beat. However, cardiac arrest will occur within a few minutes if breathing is not restored. Respiratory arrest can be caused by:

1. drowning
2. electric shock
3. suffocation
4. strangulation
5. accident
6. drug overdose
7. allergic reaction
8. infection
9. collapse of a lung
10. obstruction of the airway. (A foreign object lodged in the throat or a swelling of the airway, as happens in severe asthma or allergic reaction to bee stings, can obstruct the airway.)

In other words, respiratory arrest can be caused by anything that prevents oxygen from getting into the lungs.

Whatever the cause, if respiratory arrest is not treated immediately, cardiac arrest will occur shortly thereafter. The treatment for respiratory arrest is artificial ventilation. You will learn how to do this with the technique called mouth-to-mouth resuscitation.

Cardiac Arrest

If, in an unresponsive person, you cannot detect a pulse at the neck (carotid pulse) or heartbeat, the patient is in cardiac arrest, which can result from many accidental or medical causes. In cardiac arrest sometimes the breathing is first to fail, and at other times the pulse is first. These two events are closely related. What is important is that you recognize the symptoms of cardiac arrest so that you can begin CPR immediately.

Artificial Ventilation

It is really very simple to tell if someone is in respiratory or cardiac arrest. In both cases, the patient will be unconscious. The first thing to do is to determine if the person is unresponsive. Shake the person or tap the person on the shoulder while asking loudly, "Are you OK?" If the person makes any response, either verbal or with movement, resuscitation is not immediately necessary.

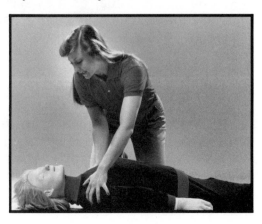

If there is no response you will need to open the airway, check to see if the person is breathing and call out for help if someone else is near enough to hear your calling out.

The victim should be on his or her back on a hard surface. If not already on his back, the victim should be rolled as gently as possible into this position. Turn him as a unit. Try to avoid twisting or bending the neck.

Once the patient is on his or her back, if no neck injury is suspected you can open the airway with a simple method called the head tilt/chin lift maneuver.

1. Kneel at the patient's side.
2. Place the hand nearest the person's head on the forehead and apply firm pressure.
3. With the other hand, place the fingers under the bony portion of the lower jaw and gently pull up, (*do not* push on the soft fleshy part) while maintaining the pressure on the forehead with your first hand.

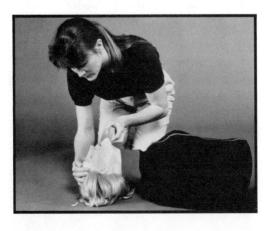

The victim's head will tilt back with their mouth

open, and their chin will be slightly elevated. Be sure the mouth is kept open.

Should you have any difficulty in keeping the mouth open and the jaw elevated, the head tilt/chin lift can also be done by grasping the jaw bone between your thumb and fingers.

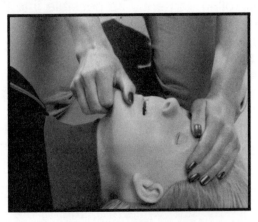

Often, this technique makes it easier to maintain an open airway and proper jaw position.

Next, in order to determine if the person is

breathing, while maintaining the head tilt/chin lift, place your ear next to the victim's mouth and your hand on the victim's chest. Now look, listen, and feel for breathing. If the person is breathing you will see the chest rise, and you will hear and feel air going in and out of the mouth and nose.

Sometimes simply opening the airway is all that is needed for breathing to resume. One of the most common causes of airway obstruction is the tongue. When a person is unconscious the muscles relax the lower jaw (to which the tongue is attached) drops back. This causes the back of the tongue, where it is attached at the floor of the mouth, to obstruct the airway. Tilting the head back will move the tongue out of the way. If an unconscious victim is breathing, maintain the open airway with head tilt/chin lift and have someone call for the ambulance.

Other Methods for Opening the Airway

Sometimes the head tilt/chin lift will not be effective. If this is the case, the jaw thrust can be used.

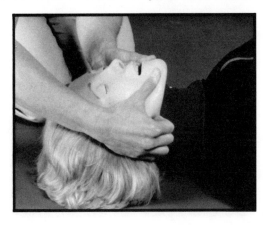

The additional forward movement of the jaw created by this method may help the airway to open.

    1. Grasp the angles of the lower jaw, lifting with both hands, while tilting the head backward.

    2. If the lips close, the lower lip can be pushed open with the thumb or fingers.

This method is more difficult and should only be attempted when the head tilt/chin lift fails. If the victim has been injured in an accident or fall from a height, the jaw thrust technique *without* any head-tilt is the correct method to use because it can be accomplished without moving or extending the neck. Spine injury must be suspected in any patient who has been injured and extending the head (tilting it back) could cause irreparable damage. The jaw thrust method can be done while holding the head still in a neutral position.

Whichever airway method you use, once the airway is open, check for breathing: look, listen, and feel. If the victim is not breathing, you must begin artificial ventilation.

Artificial Ventilation: Adults

Once the airway is open, follow these steps to perform mouth-to-mouth artificial ventilation.

1. While keeping the airway open, pinch the victim's nostrils shut using the thumb and index finger of the hand on the victim's forehead.
2. Keeping the nostrils pinched, take a deep breath, seal your mouth over the victim's mouth and slowly blow a good full breath into the victim's mouth.

3. Next remove your mouth from the victim's to let him exhale. Take a deep breath yourself. Keeping the nostrils pinched, again seal your mouth over the victim's and blow a second slow deep breath into the victim's mouth. The appropriate time for the two breaths is 1—1.5 seconds per breath. (If the victim has dentures, and they cause a problem, they should be removed.)

4. Check for a pulse. Feel for the victim's neck pulse, which can be felt in the large artery in the neck, called the carotid artery. Use the tips of your index and middle fingers to locate the center of the throat. Then slide your fingers across the neck down into the groove between the windpipe and the large muscle at the side of the neck. In this groove is the carotid artery. Feel this pulse gently—don't press too hard. Try this on yourself; you will see that it takes very little pressure to locate the pulse. Checking for a pulse should only take about five seconds. You don't need to count the pulse—just verify its presence. There is a carotid artery on either side of the neck. If the victim's carotid pulse is absent on one side, check the other side, just to be sure. Never check both carotid arteries at the same time. This could cause blood flow to the brain to be shut off.

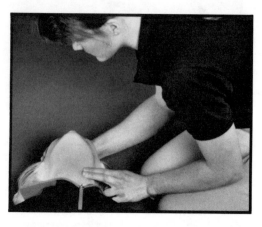

5. **If a pulse is present,** but the victim is not breathing, you will have to continue mouth-to-mouth ventilation. Pinch the nostrils again and give *one breath every five seconds—about twelve per minute.*
6. Between breaths, allow the patient to fully exhale. Watch the chest rise as you blow in, and fall when you remove your mouth and the victim exhales. Exhalation takes about three times as long as the time required for inhalation (blowing the air in).
7. Check the pulse every few minutes to be sure it is still present. Even though you have found a pulse earlier, it is necessary to continue checking so you will know immediately if the patient's heart stops (cardiac arrest).

You will know you are getting air into the patient's lungs if you see the chest rise and fall, and if you hear or feel air being exhaled. If this is not happening, try repositioning the head and chin to open the airway. If after two attempts at opening the airway you are still unable to blow air in and obtain chest rise, one of two problems exists:

1. If when you blow in the air escapes, you are not making a proper seal at the mouth or pinching the nostrils shut.
2. If you are holding the nostrils shut and have a proper seal and *can not blow air in,* the airway is obstructed and you will have to do the *unconscious obstructed airway maneuvers.* These are described later in this text.

Special Ventilation Problems

There may be times when injury to the victim's mouth and face prevent you from getting a good seal with your mouth. In such cases, you can ventilate the victim using the mouth-to-nose methods. Tilt the head back as before, hold the victim's mouth closed by lifting on the lower jaw, and place your mouth over the victim's nose. Deliver the breaths as before, and allow the victim to exhale by removing your mouth and opening the victim's mouth.

There are two special situations in which mouth-to-mouth ventilation does not work—when patients do not breathe through their nose or mouth, but through a hole in the trachea called a stoma. The first situation is the patient who has had a tracheostomy—a temporary opening (stoma) in the trachea; the second is the patient who has had a laryngectomy—removal of the larynx.

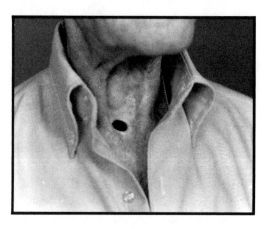

If, when you attempt to ventilate a patient, the chest does not rise and there is no sign that air is entering the lungs, and you can find no indication of airway obstruction, you should look for a stoma. When a stoma is found, you should provide mouth-to-stoma ventilation. The victim's head need not be tilted back, but the neck should be kept in a straight line. Provide ventilations at the rate of one every five seconds—twelve per minute—just as before. With a patient who has a laryngectomy it will not be necessary to seal the mouth and nose. However, if you are giving mouth-to-stoma ventilation and the chest does not rise, you should suspect a tracheostomy and use one hand to seal the mouth and nose, so that air will not escape.

Any time you give artificial ventilation or CPR, be prepared for the victim to vomit. When this happens, the liquid and solid contents of the stomach can enter the airway and obstruct it. The contents may also be aspirated—inhaled—into the lungs, where stomach acid can cause extensive, if not fatal, damage. You must turn the patient on his or her side and clean the mouth and nose of vomit before you resume ventilations. *It is very important to prevent gastric contents from obstructing the airway or entering the lungs.*

When you have given artificial ventilation for some time, you may see gastric distention—bulging of the stomach. This happens because when you blow into the victim's mouth, some of the air enters the stomach, causing it to inflate. Generally, gastric distention can be ignored. When it becomes severe, however, the diaphragm becomes elevated, putting pressure on the lungs making it impossible to ventilate effectively. It also increases the likelihood of vomiting. By giving the two breaths at a slow rate the probability of causing gastric distention will be less.

Severe gastric distention that reduces the ability to ventilate the victim should be relieved. Turn the patient on his or her side and press gently on the abdomen above the navel. Be careful to keep the patient's head to the side and angled slightly down, so gastric contents will flow out of the mouth and not be aspirated. After the distention is relieved the patient's mouth should be cleared and resuscitation continued. You should interrupt resuscitation as little as possible.

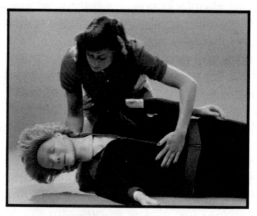

Summary (Ventilation)

In the past few pages, several methods for opening the airway and several special problems you may encounter have been presented. It is important to note that they are not usual. Even though you need to know of them, in most cases the simple head tilt/chin lift maneuver will open the airway and you will be able to ventilate the victim with mouth-to-mouth breathing without any difficulty.

Adult Artificial Ventilation Summary

Now let's review the steps in mouth-to-mouth ventilation:

1. Check for responsiveness.

2. Open the airway.

3. Look, listen, and feel for breathing.

4. If there is *no* breathing give two full breaths at 1–1.5 seconds per inspiration.

5. Check the carotid pulse.

6. If present, continue ventilations. While maintaining the open airway, give one breath every five seconds: twelve per minute.

7. Recheck the pulse every few minutes.

You furnish what the victim needs. Any unconscious patient needs to have his airway kept open. If, once the airway is opened he breathes for himself, you maintain the airway. If he is not breathing for himself, open the airway and provide ventilation.

Cardiopulmonary Resuscitation—CPR: Adult

In an unresponsive, non-breathing victim, keeping the airway open and giving mouth-to-mouth ventilation provides oxygen to the lungs. The presence of a carotid pulse indicates that the victim has adequate heart beat and circulation to get the oxygen to the body cells. If *NO* carotid pulse is present the patient is in both respiratory and cardiac arrest. Ventilation alone is not enough. You will also have to provide artificial circulation.

Artificial circulation can be provided by the use of proper chest compressions. Chest compressions increase the air pressure within the chest, thereby causing blood to surge from the chest throughout the body with each compression. When you release pressure on the chest the blood vessels refill. By compressing and releasing you provide artificial circulation. It is impossible to inflate the lungs (blow into the victim) and compress the chest at the same time, therefore ventilations and chest compressions are alternated. Each must be performed properly. Good ventilations remain key in order that the compressions circulate properly oxygenated blood to the body cells.

Alternately providing artificial ventilation and chest compressions is called Cardiopulmonary Resuscitation, or more simply—CPR.

The sequence is the same as you have learned—check responsiveness, open the airway (head tilt/chin lift), and check for breathing. If none is present, squeeze the nostrils shut and provide two slow breaths using mouth-to-mouth, then check for the presence of a carotid pulse. If *no* pulse is present start chest compressions, then alternate between ventilating the patient and providing chest progressions. *Never* do chest compressions on someone who is responsive or has a carotid pulse.

The following pages detail the correct way to provide artificial circulation and the correct rate and intervals for alternating between ventilations and chest compressions.

Chest Compressions

Chest compressions must be given correctly—this involves more than just pushing on the chest.

First, the victim must be on his or her back on a hard surface—such as the floor or ground. If the victim is in a chair or in bed, he or she must be dragged to the floor. No other position will allow you to give effective CPR.

In order to give chest compressions, first bare the chest. This will help you see where to place your hands. Open the shirt, get any underwear out of the way, or cut through or push up a bra if necessary. Don't let modesty or embarrassment prevent you from doing your job properly.

Kneel next to the patient's chest so that your knees are as close as possible to the patient's side. Now follow these steps:

1. With the middle and index fingers of the hand closest to the patient's navel, feel the lower edge of the rib cage.
2. Follow along the edge of the ribs to the

notch in the midline of the chest, where
the ribs join the sternum.

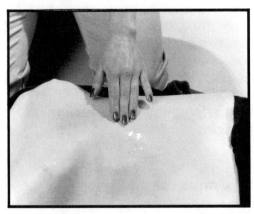

3. Locate the notch with your middle finger.
   The index finger is placed next to this finger at the lower end of the sternum.
4. Place only the heel of your other hand directly on the sternum, so that it touches
   the index finger of the landmark hand.

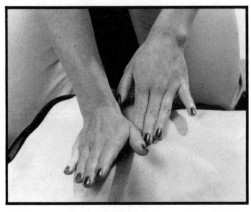

5. Now remove the landmark hand and place

it directly on top of the other hand so that both hands are parallel to each other. Remember, only the heel of your bottom hand should be touching the patient. Be sure your fingers are not touching the chest. This could cause ribs to be fractured when pressure is exerted. (Interlacing your fingers will help to avoid touching the chest.) This "landmarking" assures that your hand position is correct for compressions and is higher than the sharp *Xiphoid Process* located at the lower end of the sternum. Compressing on the Xiphoid can cause internal injury.

6. Because of varying sizes of people's hands, an alternate acceptable method for holding the hands is to grasp the wrist of the hand on the chest with the hand that had located the sternal notch. Rescuers who suffer from arthritis may find comfort with this style.

7. Be sure that your knees are in close to the patient's side. Your shoulders and arms should be directly over the patient's sternum, and *your elbows should be locked straight.*

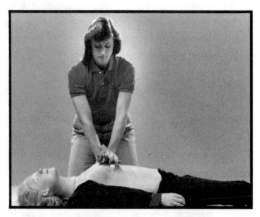

8. Use the weight of your body to exert force while keeping your elbows locked. Drive down on the sternum so that you compress the chest one-and-one half to two inches.

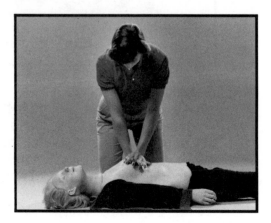

9. Compress the chest for less than a second. Then allow it to rise to its normal position and be ready to compress again, but don't take your hands off the chest. Avoid bouncing or rocking the chest. You must compress and release the chest at a rate of 80 to 100 times per minute. Count out loud: "One-and-two-and-three-and-four-and-five-and-six-and-seven-and-eight-and-nine-and-ten-and-eleven-and-twelve-and-thirteen-and-fourteen-and-fifteen".
10. When you have completed fifteen compressions, quickly move to the head. Open the airway, and give two quick, full breaths.
11. Return to the chest, locate the landmark, and position your hands one on top of the other, correctly.
12. Give fifteen compressions.
13. Continue compressions and ventilations at the rate of fifteen compressions to two ventilations.

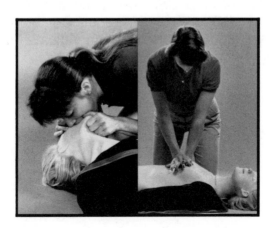

Recheck the carotid pulse every few minutes. To do this, CPR must be interrupted so that you don't feel the surge of blood caused by your compressions. But don't stop for more than five seconds. Check the pulse after giving the two breaths. If there is *no pulse,* give two additional breaths and continue compressions and ventilations as before. One way to tell if your CPR is effective is to look at the eyelids, or inside the lips or at the fingernail beds, to see if a pink color has returned. Remember, once CPR has begun, don't stop. Continue until professional help arrives.

Continuing CPR

It is important to continue CPR without interruption except for the periodic checking for the carotid pulse. Should a carotid pulse return, continue maintaining the airway and providing ventilations until either the patient breathes for himself or again goes into cardiac arrest—requiring the reinstitution of CPR.

Do not stop CPR when the ambulance arrives and the EMT's enter the room. Continue CPR until they are ready to take over and indicate that they are ready to replace you.

Adult CPR Summary

Now let's review the steps of one-operator CPR (adult victim) from the beginning:

1. Check for responsiveness.
2. Turn victim on his back as a unit, call for help.
3. Open the airway.
4. Look, listen, and feel for breathing.
5. Give two full breaths, at 1-1.5 seconds per breath.
6. Check the carotid pulse. Once you have determined that the victim is in cardiac arrest, get someone to call the ambulance. If you are alone you will have to call for help and begin CPR.
7. Bare the chest.
8. Find the landmark and position your hands correctly on the chest.
9. Give fifteen chest compressions, at the rate of 80-100 compressions per minute.
10. Open the airway and give two ventilations.
11. Continue alternating, fifteen compressions and two ventilations until help arrives.
12. Every few minutes, after a ventilation, stop CPR and check for the presence of a carotid pulse. If none is present continue CPR.

Different CPR Techniques

Medical personnel and Emergency Responders are trained in several methods for delivering CPR. When responding as a team to an emergency they will often use a different method than you have been taught. They will provide two operator manual CPR, in which one operator provides ventilation and the other performs chest compressions. *Do not be alarmed at this difference in method.*

Artificial Ventilation and CPR: Children and Infants

For rescusitation purposes, children are classified into three groups:
1. Children with a body size larger than the average eight year old.
2. Children with a body size between that of a one year old and that of an eight year old.
3. Infants, from birth to one year old.

Children Over Eight Years of Age: Artificial Ventilation and CPR

With any child whose body size is over that of an eight year old, open the airway and provide artificial ventilation or give CPR following the same method as for an adult.

Simply stated:

In Children over eight, use adult ventilation and CPR techniques.

Artificial Ventilation: Children One Year to Eight Years Old.

Artificial ventilation for children (except infants) is done in the same way as in an adult:

1. Check for responsiveness.
2. If child is not on his back, roll him over as a unit and place him on a hard surface.
3. Kneel next to the victim's head.
4. Open the airway by head tilt/chin lift.
   Note:
   If spine injury is suspected, hold the head in a straight neutral position (without head tilt) and use the jaw thrust technique.
5. While maintaining the open airway, *Look, Listen and Feel* for breathing (air movement, chest rise.)

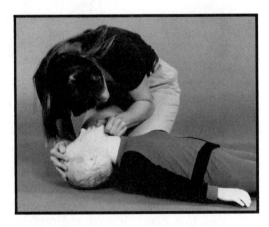

6. With the hand on the forehead, pinch the nostrils closed.

7. Maintaining the open airway, seal your mouth over the victim's mouth and deliver two slow breaths (1–1.5 second/inspirations). In smaller children less volume will be necessary than for adults, watch chest rise as the indicator of when adequate volume is blown into the child's mouth. Excessive volume will cause gastric distention.

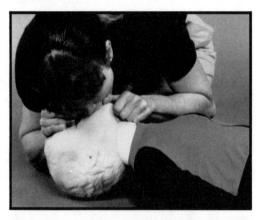

8. While maintaining the head tilt with one hand check for the presence of a carotid pulse with the other hand. Call for help.
9. *If a carotid pulse is present* but the victim is not breathing, continue mouth-to-mouth ventilations. Maintain the head tilt with your hand on the forehead, and pinch the nostrils shut. Replace your other hand under the chin. While maintaining an open airway with the head tilt/chin lift, *give one breath every five seconds (about twelve per minute).*

10. Between breaths, allow the patient to exhale fully.
11. While maintaining the head tilt, stop ventilations and recheck the carotid pulse every few minutes.

Child (1–8 yr.) Artificial Ventilation Summary

Let's review the steps:

1. Check for Responsiveness.
2. Roll child as a unit, place on his back on a firm, hard surface.
3. Open airway with head tilt/chin lift.
4. Look, Listen and Feel for breathing while maintaining the open airway.
5. Pinch nostrils closed.
6. Provide two slow ventilations, sealing mouth over victim's mouth and maintaining open airway.
7. Maintaining head tilt with one hand, check for presence of a carotid pulse with the other.
8. *If a carotid pulse is present,* but victim is *not breathing,* provide head tilt/chin lift and ventilate patient with *one breath every five seconds (12 breaths per minute).*
9. Check the carotid pulse every few minutes while maintaining the head tilt (one hand on forehead).

CPR: Children One Year to Eight Years Old

If in an unresponsive, non-breathing child *No carotid pulse is present,* the child is in cardiac arrest and needs CPR.

The general principles of CPR—alternating ventilations with chest compressions—remain the same as for adults. However, the method of performing chest compressions is modified and the number of compressions and ventilations is changed because of the child's smaller size.

Once you have:

1. Checked for Responsiveness.

2. Called for help and positioned the victim on his back on a hard surface.

3. Opened the airway with head tilt/chin lift.

4. Checked (Look, Listen, and Feel) for breathlessness.

5. Provided two slow breaths while maintaining head tilt/chin lift.

6. While maintaining the head tilt, checked the carotid pulse.

If no pulse is present, you will want to go on to perform chest compressions and then alternate ventilations.

Chest Compressions: Children 1–8 Years Old

1. Move so that you are kneeling alongside the child's chest.
2. Bare the chest
3. While maintaining head tilt with your hand closest to the child's head, locate the edge of the rib cage with your other hand (the one closest to the child's feet). With the middle and index fingers feel the edge of the ribs. Follow along the edge of the ribs to the notch in the middle of the chest, where the ribs join the sternum. Locate the notch with your middle finger. The index finger is placed next to this finger at the lower edge of the sternum. Look at your hand and the chest—this represents the "landmark" position.

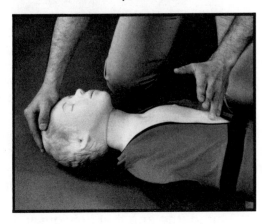

4. Lift the hand off the chest and place the heel of your same hand on the midline of the sternum, so that it is on the chest just above the point where the index finger was. Be sure you are higher than this point and *Not directly over the Xiphoid.*

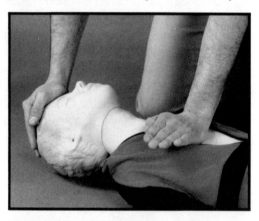

5. Note that your other hand remains on the forehead maintaining the head tilt. With one hand only, deliver *five compressions* at a rate of 80 to 100 compressions per minute.   ("One-and-two-and-three-and-four-and-five")

In a child, the chest should be compressed between one and one and a half inches. This is slightly less than in an adult.

6. While maintaining the head tilt, slide up near the victim's head and place your free hand (the one that previously did the compressions) at the chin to effect the head tilt/chin lift.

7. Seal your mouth over the victim's and deliver one ventilation.

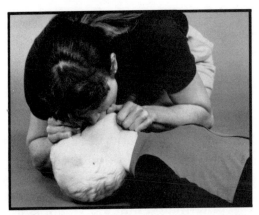

8. While maintaining the head tilt, look at the midline of the chest and, from memory, replace the palm of your hand on the chest where it was previously placed. Be sure that you have *not* placed it over the Xiphoid.
9. Deliver five one-handed compressions, then one ventilation, then five compressions, then one ventilation, etc.
(Note that the hand nearest the victim's head remains on the forehead maintaining the head tilt, your other hand alternates between the chest when giving compressions and the chin lift when ventilating.)
10. Every few minutes, while maintaining the head tilt with one hand, stop CPR and check for the presence of a carotid pulse.
11. IF the pulse is *not* present, continue CPR.

Child CPR Summary (1–8 years)

Now let's review the steps of one-operator CPR (child victim) from the beginning:

1. Check for responsiveness.
2. Turn victim on his back as a unit, call for help.
3. Open the airway.
4. Look, Listen and Feel for breathing (maintain head tilt/chin lift).
5. Give two slow breaths.
6. Check the carotid pulse. Once you have determined that the victim is in cardiac arrest, have someone call the ambulance.
7. Bare the chest.
8. While maintaining the head tilt with one hand, slide down next to the chest. Find the landmark, and position your hand correctly on the sternum *(be sure you are not on the Xiphoid).*
9. Give five one-handed compressions (compressing the chest 1 to 1 $1/2$ inches).
10. Replace hand on chin, perform head tilt/chin lift, ventilate once.
11. While maintaining head tilt with one hand, replace the other hand on the chest and deliver five compressions.
12. Continue alternating one ventilation and five chest compressions.
13. Every few minutes, stop CPR and recheck for the presence of a carotid pulse.
14. If none is present, continue CPR until the EMTs arrive and take over.

Artificial Ventilation and CPR: Infants (0–12 Months)

Due to an infant's small size and other anatomical differences, artificial ventilation and CPR although following the same principles as for a child, employ altered techniques for opening the airway, ventilation and chest compressions.

Artificial Ventilation: Infant (0–12 Months)

1. First establish if the infant is conscious or unresponsive. To establish responsiveness, tap or gently shake a shoulder. Snapping your fingers against the infant's foot is another good method.
2. Using both hands, pick-up the infant. Turn him on his back while supporting the head and neck. Place him on a firm hard surface and call out for help.
3. Use head tilt/chin lift to open the airway. When opening the airway of an infant, you must be very careful *not* to extend the head and neck as much as you would with an adult. This fully extended position may obstruct the infant's airway, since the trachea of an infant is so flexible. The head tilt in an infant should be limited so that the head is only mildly tilted. The chin is held as in an adult or child. Be careful that your fingers do not push into the soft flesh under the infant's chin, closing the infant's trachea (windpipe).

4. Look, Listen and feel for breathing. In infants, chest movement and abdominal movement occur with breathing.

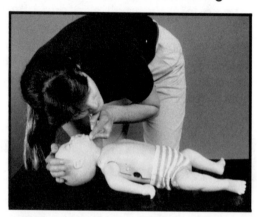

5. While keeping the airway open, seal your mouth over the infant's *nose and mouth* and blow in a small breath. The amount that is necessary will depend upon the infants size. You can tell when you have blown in enough by watching (out of the corner of your eye) the chest rise and by feel.

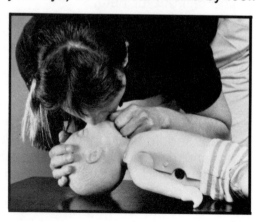

6. Remove your mouth and take a breath. Again seal your mouth over the infant's mouth and nose and deliver a second breath.
7. Maintain the mild head tilt with the hand closest to the top of the infant's head, and with the other hand raise the infant's arm closest to you up over the infant's head. In infants the carotid pulse (in the neck) is *not* used since it is very difficult to locate in the soft, short neck. Instead the brachial pulse is used. To take the brachial pulse, place the tips of your three long fingers on the inside of the baby's upper arm, between the elbow and armpit. Press gently until you feel a pulse. You can get an idea of this by taking your own brachial pulse, in the same place. Do not use your thumb when taking a pulse. It has a pulse of its own, and you may feel it instead of the pulse you are trying to obtain. Have someone call the ambulance.

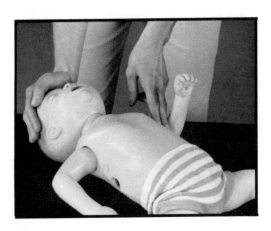

8. If a pulse is present, replace your hand at the chin and continue giving artificial ventilation. In an infant, breaths are provided *every three seconds: twenty per minute.*
9. While maintaining the mild head tilt, every few minutes recheck the brachial pulse.

Infant Artificial Ventilation Summary

Let's review the steps:
1. Check responsiveness.
2. While supporting the head and neck, pick up the infant and place on a hard firm surface face-up.
3. Do head tilt/chin lift (mild head tilt or to "sniffing" position.)
4. Look, Listen and Feel for breathing while maintaining head tilt/chin lift.
5. If *not breathing,* provide two slow breaths by sealing your mouth over the infant's nose and mouth and maintaining the head tilt/chin lift.
6. Maintaining head tilt with one hand on forehead, raise infant's arm over his head and check for presence of a brachial pulse.
7. *If pulse is present,* continue giving artificial ventilation. Provide breaths *every three seconds (20 per minute)* while maintaining head tilt/chin lift.
8. Every few minutes recheck for the presence of a brachial pulse while maintaining the head tilt, with the other hand.

CPR: Infants (0–12 months)

If in an unresponsive non-breathing infant *no brachial pulse is present,* the infant is in cardiac arrest and needs CPR.

The general principles of CPR, alternating one breath and five chest compressions, remain the same as for children. The method of giving compressions and maintaining the proper rate is different because of the small size of an infant.

Once you have:

1. Checked for responsiveness

2. Called out for help and positioned the infant on his back on a hard surface

3. Opened the airway with mild head tilt/chin lift

4. Checked (Look, Listen and Feel) for breathlessness

5. Provided two slow breaths

6. While maintaining head tilt, have checked the brachial pulse (felt in the underside of the upper arm)

If *no pulse is present,* you will want to go on to perform chest compressions and then alternately ventilate.

Chest Compressions: Infant 0–12 months

1. Bare the chest.
2. While maintaining head tilt with the hand closest to the top of the child's head, visualize an imaginary line between the nipples. Place two to three fingers *one finger's-width below* this imaginary line—on the midline of the sternum.

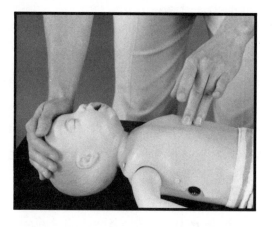

3. Deliver five compressions at a rate of one hundred compressions per minute ("One-two-three-four-five"). In an infant the chest should be compressed *between one-half to one inch.* Do not take your hand off the infant's chest.
4. Using only the head tilt and leaving the lower hand on the chest, deliver one breath.

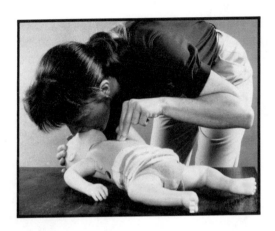

Important Note

The *airway in most infants can be maintained for CPR with just head tilt.* In order to provide five compressions and alternately one ventilation continuously, so that at the end of a minute one hundred compressions and twenty ventilations in all have been delivered, great speed is required. Repositioning of the hand from the chest to the chin and back to the chest (as is done with children) is too time consuming and reduces the possible rate of compressions; therefore it is not done unless necessary in infants. *In the event that you have difficulty maintaining the airway with just head tilt, you will (as in a child victim) have to move the hand from the chest to the chin to provide chin lift at each ventilation, and carefully reposition the hand on the chest prior to delivering the five compressions.* In this case you will physically not be able to deliver correct compressions at a rate much over fifty per minute. (Policy of Pediat-

ric Working Group of the Emergency Cardiac Care
Committee of the American Heart Association)
>   5. Alternate delivering five compressions and
>   then one breath.

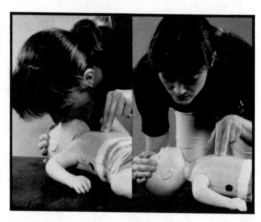

>   6. Maintaining the head tilt, every few minutes
>   stop CPR and recheck for the presence of a
>   brachial pulse.
>   7. If *No pulse* is present, continue CPR.

Infant (0–12 Months) CPR Summary

Now let's review the steps of Infant CPR from the
beginning:
>   1. Check for responsiveness.
>   2. Turn victim on his back as a unit
>   3. Open airway using mild head tilt/chin lift.
>   (remember, do not over-extend the head).

4. Look, Listen and Feel for breathing, while maintaining an open airway.
5. Give two slow breaths by sealing your mouth over infant's *mouth and nose* and maintaining the open airway.
6. Maintaining the head tilt, check the brachial pulse. Once you have determined that the victim is in cardiac arrest, have someone call the ambulance.
7. Bare the chest.
8. While maintaining head tilt with one hand, place two to three fingers of the other hand one finger's-width lower than an imaginary line between the nipples—on the midline of the sternum.
9. Deliver five compressions, compressing the chest $1/2$ to 1 inch.
10. Without removing the hand on the forehead (maintaining the head tilt) and keeping the other hand on the chest, alternate between one breath and five compressions at a rate of one hundred compressions per minute.

(Note—only if you can not maintain the airway should you move the hand off the chest to perform chin lift with ventilation).

11. Every few minutes stop CPR and recheck the brachial pulse while maintaining the head tilt.
12. If *no pulse is present,* continue CPR.

Conclusion: Artificial Ventilation and CPR

Remember Artificial Ventilation must be started immediately after recognizing that the victim *is not breathing.* CPR must be started immediately after cardiac arrest is recognized. You provide what the unresponsive victim needs.

> If he is not breathing—because he can not keep his airway open—you open the airway. In many unresponsive patients this may be all that is necessary to restore spontaneous breathing.

> If, when you open the airway the victim is not breathing but has a pulse, you provide artificial ventilation.

> If he is unresponsive, has no respiration, and is in cardiac arrest, you perform CPR. With CPR you provide an airway, breathing, and circulation for the victim.

Once started, CPR must be continued until you are relieved by the EMT's and they are ready to take over, or the patient's pulse returns. Remember, CPR must be stopped for a few seconds while you are checking the pulse. While compressions are being given there will be a pulse. It indicates that proper compressions are being given, *Not* that the patient has a heart beat.

If when you stop CPR and check, a pulse is present, stop giving CPR and provide only mouth-to-mouth ventilation. Every few minutes recheck the pulse. Should it be absent, reinstitute CPR.

If the victim's pulse returns and they regain spontaneous breathing, maintain the airway and monitor their breathing. If it stops, reinstitute artificial ventilation and check the pulse. Provide ventilation or CPR as needed.

Simply stated:

- Unconscious unresponsive victims need to be placed on their back on a firm surface— and need to have their airway maintained open by the rescuer (chin lift/head tilt or if the patient is injured, jaw thrust with the head not moved and held in a neutral inline position.)
- Once the airway is opened, if the patient is not breathing but has a pulse, they need artificial ventilation.
- Once the airway is opened, if the patient is not breathing and has *no pulse,* they need CPR to provide both ventilation and circulation.

Any victim who is either in respiratory arrest or cardiac arrest immediately needs you to start the appropriate rescusitation. They also rapidly need Advanced Care. Therefore, it is important that the Emergency Ambulance be summoned without delay.

If you are one of several people present you can immediately begin ventilation or CPR and, by calling out for help, summon another household member. Then they can without delay call the Emergency Ambulance, meet the EMT's at the door, and rapidly guide them to your exact location.

If you are alone with the victim or your location is such that no one responds to your call for "Help!", you should first focus on the victim. After having instituted ventilation or CPR and providing it for two to three minutes you will have to deal with calling for the emergency ambulance. If the victim is a child or infant, discontinuing rescusitation for a few seconds and carrying the victim to a telephone is recommended. Reinstitute CPR and then, after several cycles, interrupt it for a few seconds while you call.

If the victim is a large adult you will have to determine whether dragging the victim to the phone is possible (If he is not injured). It may not be practical, or you may decide less interruption and time loss without CPR would occur (after initiating CPR for two-three minutes), by stopping CPR while you go to the phone and call for the emergency ambulance.

If any situation where you have to interrupt CPR in order to go to the phone and call for the ambulance:

- Don't run.
- Be calm—and don't talk faster than the dispatcher can write.
- Immediately tell the dispatcher that the victim is in arrest, that you have started CPR, and that you have interrupted CPR in order to call.
- Be brief, but give *all necessary information* to ensure the ambulance can find your location.
- If the victim is on a second floor, in the backyard, in the cellar—or any location where you and the victim will not be obvious to the arriving EMT's, be sure to give the dispatcher that information also.
- When returning to the victim, re-open the airway and re-institute CPR starting with two breaths.

When you are at home alone with the victim, an additional problem may be presented by the front door being locked (ambulance personnel will not be able to get in). *Do not* continue the interruption caused by telephoning for the Emergency Ambulance in order to go and unlock the front door.

Instead:

- Initiate CPR
- Interrupt CPR to call, tell the dispatcher that the front door will be unlocked and exactly where you will be ("upstairs" or "on the back porch" etc.)
- Reinstitute CPR for two to three minutes.
- Interrupt CPR to unlock front door.
- Reinstitute CPR and continue it until the EMT's are ready to take over.

One last, very important point to remember. Not everyone in cardiac arrest can be saved, even if you give perfect CPR. Often the initial medical cause or mechanism of injury resulting in Cardiac Arrest has caused so much damage (cell death) that saving the victim simply is not possible. Even when patients arrest in the hospital or in a Paramedic Ambulance, where a team is present to provide CPR and Advanced Life Support (IV's, cardiac drugs, electrical pacing to stimulate the heart, etc.), the number that survive an arrest is a relatively small percent. You should not feel discouraged or guilty if the victim dies. What is important is that you gave the victim a chance for life, *if* he or she was saveable.

If your timely starting of CPR and the ensuing efforts of the EMT's and the emergency staff at the hospital failed to save the patient, you and his or her survivors will at least know that everything that was medically possible was done. Although this can not counter the loss of a loved one, it should provide substantial comfort.

CPR has the highest save rate in victims who have good health and have not had long term problems and years of physical deterioration. Your prompt action and skills may keep such a victim from a needless death.

Airway Obstruction

Your ability to ventilate the patient (to blow air in) is dependent upon maintaining an open airway. Without a proper airway artificial ventilation or full CPR will not be effective, since you will not be able to properly ventilate and oxygenate the lungs and therefore will not be able to provide proper oxygen levels in the blood to meet the cells' needs. It is essential to have an open airway.

Three items can result in an obstructed airway:
- The victim's tongue falls back, causing a blockage.
- Fluids, blood, secretions or vomitus obstruct the airway.
- A medical condition exists causing swelling which obstructs the airway.
- A foreign body lodges in the airway and the victim can not clear it.

The most common cause of airway obstruction in unconscious victims is their tongue. When conscious, people have a gag reflex. Whenever any object (including the tongue) gets in the airway this gag reflex stimulates coughing, which prevents the object from going further and clears it out of the airway. The gag reflex and the normal muscle tone of the tongue prevent the tongue from falling back and obstructing the airway even when you are asleep. There are varying levels of unconsciousness, ranging from arousable sleep to unresponsive coma. At a given level of unconsciousness a victim loses his gag reflex and muscle tone. With the victim on his back, the limp tongue falls to the back of the mouth and shapes to obstruct the airway. The head tilt/chin lift, the head tilt/jaw thrust or the jaw thrust holding the head neutral (for injured victims where spine injury is suspected) each extends the lower jaw. This elevates the tongue, pulling it forward away from the back of the mouth and opens the airway.

Any unresponsive patient who is on his back needs to have an airway maneuver performed and maintained, to assure that the tongue can not obstruct the airway. That is why, once unresponsiveness is ascertained, an airway maneuver is performed prior to checking if the patient is breathing or not. If the tongue is the item obstructing the airway, the head tilt/chin lift (or one of the other airway maneuvers) will clear it and keep the airway open. The degree of head tilt and the amount of elevation of the jaw that is necessary to open an individual's airway will vary from person to person based upon their individual anatomy. In any victim, if the lower jaw falls back (regresses) so that the chin doesn't jut out further than the upper teeth, the tongue can obstruct the airway.

A piece of food, chewing gum, candy, a small object (a piece of a toy), etc., can become lodged in the airway causing an obstruction. When a foreign object is obstructing the airway it will not be cleared by the previously described airway maneuvers. It must be cleared using the Obstructed Airway (Choking) sequence.

Different techniques are used to clear an obstructed airway if the victim is conscious (choking) than are used if the victim is unconscious.

Airway Obstruction, Unconscious Adult or Child

The techniques for unconscious victims start the same way as the previously-taught sequences for artificial ventilation, since the problem or cause will not be known to you:

1. Check for responsiveness.
2. As a unit turn the victim on his back on a firm hard surface—call out "Help!"
3. Open the airway (head tilt-chin lift or other airway maneuver).
4. While maintaining the head tilt/chin lift, Look, Listen, and Feel for breathing.

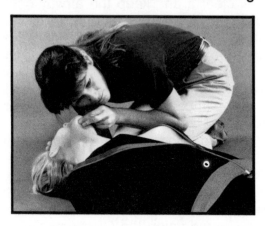

5. While maintaining the open airway, pinch the nostrils shut.
6. Seal your mouth over the victim's and attempt to ventilate.

If when you attempt to blow air into the victim you feel resistance—that is, you feel that you can not blow air in—the victim's airway is obstructed. The most common cause of failure to ventilate is improper head position, resulting in the tongue remaining as an obstruction in the airway. Therefore, next:

7. Reposition the victim's head, to obtain better head tilt and be sure that the chin lift accompanying the head tilt results in the mouth being open and the jaw being properly elevated (you may have to grasp the chin between your thumb and fingers to ensure this.)

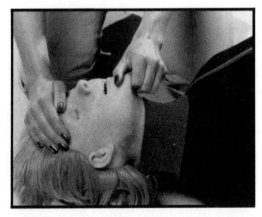

8. While maintaining the head tilt/chin lift, pinch the nostrils shut and *reattempt to ventilate.*

If you can ventilate, the tongue was the problem and has now been cleared. Provide a second slow breath, and check the carotid pulse. If the pulse is present, continue to provide ventilations; if the pulse is absent, provide CPR.

If you *still can not ventilate,* continue the obstructed airway procedure:

9. Kneel next to the victim's thighs facing the victim's head, or straddle the victim (Select which is easier and quicker). Have someone call for the ambulance.
10. Locate the victim's navel and the bottom of the sternum. Place one hand against the abdomen in the midline, slightly above the navel and well below the tip of the xiphoid. Place the second hand directly on top of the first.

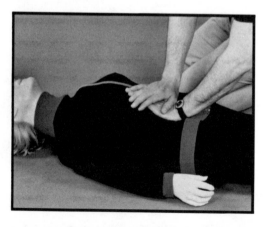

11. Press into the abdomen with quick, upward thrusts. Perform six to ten distinct abdominal thrusts.
12. Move to the victim's head, place your

thumb in the mouth on the tongue. Grasp the tongue and chin between the thumb and fingers and elevate the chin as shown below. This tongue-jaw lift will open the mouth widely.

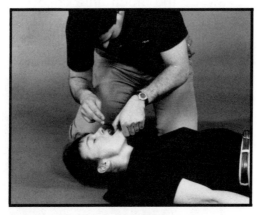

13. In an adult (only), look into the mouth and using two fingers of the other hand sweep deeply into the mouth to remove any foreign body.

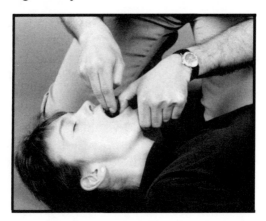

Never sweep the mouth in a child or Infant. In a child, perform the tongue-jaw lift and look carefully into the mouth—remove any object you can visualize. Be careful not to push the object deeper. Remember, never sweep the mouth in a child.

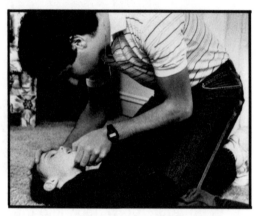

14. Do head tilt/chin lift and attempt to ventilate.
15. If you can still *not ventilate,* repeat steps 9 thru 14:
    - Six to Ten abdominal thrusts.
    - Tongue-jaw lift.
      —in an adult sweep mouth
      —in a child visualize mouth (Do Not Sweep)
    - Head tilt/chin lift.
    - Attempt to ventilate.
    Continue repeating these steps until you are successful or until the EMT's arrive and take over.

Do not be discouraged if you are not immediately successful. Often, rescuers are successful after repeated attempts as the victim's level of unconsciousness deepens. If you can ventilate the patient, you will know you have successfully cleared the airway. Once the airway obstruction has been cleared, keep the airway open and if the patient is not breathing provide artificial ventilation, or if they are unresponsive and not breathing and do *not have a carotid pulse,* provide CPR.

Obstructed Airway: Unconscious Pregnant Victim

If the victim with a foreign body obstruction is pregnant you should follow the same steps as for any unconscious patient, except *Do not do abdominal thrusts* as they could be dangerous to both mother and child. Instead, abdominal thrusts are replaced by slow chest compressions delivered in the same place and hand position as CPR, but slower and each a distinct forceful compression.

Unconscious Adult or Child Obstructed Airway Summary

Let's review the steps in clearing a foreign body obstruction in an Unconscious Adult or Child:
1. Check for responsiveness. Call out "Help!".
2. Turn victim as a unit on his back on a firm hard surface.

3. Do head tilt/chin lift airway maneuver.
4. Look, Listen and Feel for Non-Breathing while maintaining head tilt/chin lift.
5. Pinch nostrils shut, seal mouth over victim's mouth and attempt to ventilate while maintaining head tilt/chin lift.

If you cannot ventilate:
6. Reposition head, increase chin lift, and again attempt to ventilate.
7. Have someone call for the ambulance.

If you are still unable to ventilate:
8. Move next to victim's thighs, face victim's head (or straddle victim's thighs).
9. Place heel of one hand against victim's abdomen (in the midline) slightly above the navel and well below the tip of the Xiphoid. Place the second hand directly on top of the first.
10. Perform six-ten abdominal thrusts (In a pregnant victim chest compressions should be used instead.)
11. Use tongue—jaw lift
    —*In an adult,* sweep the mouth.
    —*Do not sweep the mouth in a child,* instead look in and remove the object if you can visualize it.
12. Open airway with head tilt/chin lift.
13. Attempt to ventilate.

If you still cannot ventilate:
14. Repeat steps 8 to 13 until the object is cleared or until the EMT's arrive and take over.

Obstructed Airway: Unconscious Infant (0–12 Months)

The procedure for clearing a foreign body obstruction in an unconscious infant is different from the procedure used in an Adult or Child. Abdominal thrusts are *NOT* used since these would be dangerous considering the infants size and development. Instead thoracic pressure is increased to expel the object, alternately using back blows and chest compressions. The first steps are as usual in the unconscious:

1. Check for responsiveness.
2. Turn infant on back on firm hard surface. "Call out for Help".
3. Open the Airway, using head tilt/chin lift (Do not overextend the head in an infant).
4. While maintaining head tilt/chin lift: Look, Listen, and Feel for non breathing.
5. Seal your mouth over the Infant's nose and mouth. Attempt to ventilate while maintaining head tilt/chin lift.
6. If you are unable to ventilate, reposition the head into a slightly more tilted "sniffing" position. Be sure mouth is open and chin is elevated. Attempt to ventilate.
7. Have someone summon the ambulance.

If you are still unable to ventilate you must go on with the Obstructed Airway procedure:

8. Place one arm under the infant, supporting the head, neck and torso (your hand supports the head and neck and your forearm the torso.) Place your second arm over the infant. Sandwiched between your arms, pick up the infant and turn him over—so he is face down.

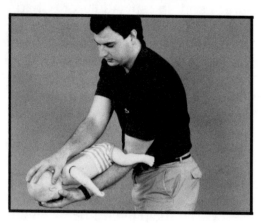

9. With the infant supported on your lower arm (legs straddling your upper arm) and his head and neck supported by your hand, and lower than the torso, place your forearm on your thigh or an immovable object. Then, with the heel of your other hand, deliver *four back blows* forcefully between the shoulder blades. Be sure that the arm under the infant is supported and can *not* move, so that the compression of the chest caused by the back blows is not lost.

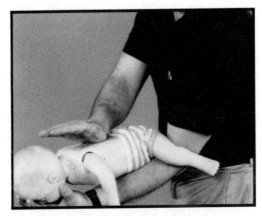

10. While supporting the head and neck, and with the infant sandwiched between your arms, turn him so he is face up.
11. With the head lower than the torso deliver four chest thrusts in the midsternal area in the same maneuver as CPR chest thrusts, but at a slower rate (three to five seconds).

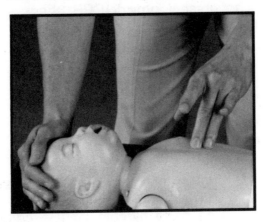

12. Do tongue-jaw lift, look into the mouth. Remove the foreign body if visualized (*Do Not sweep the mouth in an infant*).
13. Open the airway with head tilt/chin lift.
14. Seal your mouth over the infant's mouth and nose and, while maintaining head tilt/chin lift, attempt to ventilate.

If you can still not ventilate:

15. Repeat steps 8 thru 14 until you clear the obstruction (and can ventilate) or until the EMT's arrive and are ready to take over.

Do not be discouraged. Remember that often the obstruction can only be dislodged after repeated attempts and after the victim is unconscious deeply enough that the muscles totally relax.

If the object is cleared and your attempt to ventilate is successful, ventilate a second time and then, maintaining head tilt, check the brachial pulse. If the pulse is present, provide artificial ventilation until spontaneous ventilation (breathing) returns. If the pulse is *not* present, provide CPR, checking the pulse every few minutes.

Unconscious Infant Obstructed Airway Summary

1. Check for responsiveness.
2. Turn infant on back as a unit, place on firm hard surface. Call out for help.
3. Use head tilt/chin lift (Be careful not to over-extend infant's head, only to neutral or slight "sniffing" position).
4. Sealing your mouth over infant's *nose and*

mouth, and maintaining head tilt/chin lift, attempt to ventilate.

If you can not ventilate:

5. Reposition head, with slightly more head tilt and positive chin lift into "sniffing" position.
6. Re-attempt to ventilate while maintaining head tilt/chin lift.
7. Have someone call for the ambulance.

If you still can not ventilate:

8. Sandwich infant between your arms, turn him over (so he is face down), support head and neck with your hand his torso with your forearm. Support your forearm on your thigh or other immovable object.
9. Deliver four back blows forcefully between the shoulder blades with the heel of your other hand.
10. While supporting his head and neck, sandwich infant between your arms and turn (face up) onto your arm. Support your lower arm so it doesn't give.
11. Deliver four chest thrusts in midsternal region (the same as chest compressions), but slower.
12. Do tongue-jaw lift and look into the mouth. Remove foreign body if visualized. *Do not sweep mouth in an infant.*
13. Open airway with head tilt/chin lift.
14. While maintaining head tilt/chin lift, seal mouth and nose and attempt to ventilate.

If still unable to ventilate:

15. Repeat steps 8 thru 14 until obstruction is cleared (you can ventilate) or the EMT's arrive and are ready to take over.

Airway Obstruction: Conscious Victims

Victims of an obstructed airway remain conscious, even though they can not breath adequately (or at all) for a short period of time before the lack of oxygen results in unconsciousness. Airway obstruction in adults most commonly occurs when the victim is eating. For this reason it is often called a "Cafe Coronary". The possibility of this happening is greatly increased if the person is talking and eating at the same time. Alcohol, which slows the gag reflex (the reflex that causes rapid coughing to expel an object), may also contribute to this kind of airway obstruction. In adults the object is usually a piece of poorly chewed, shapeable meat (such as rare roast beef) or a multiply pointed, rigid item such as a triangular chip, piece of celery, or raw carrot. In children it is most often an item such as a piece of hot dog, round candies, nuts, or grapes, or a piece of a toy such as the eye of a stuffed doll or a marble, or coin, or other non-food object.

Obstruction occurs when the item is aspirated into the trachea (windpipe) and becomes lodged there. This is an accute emergency. If the airway is totally obstructed, or so substantially obstructed that significant air passage is blocked, the person will die unless you act quickly.

Complete Obstruction

The fully obstructed victim will be unable to speak, cough, or move air (breathe). Grunting sounds can be generated from the diaphragm but no "vocal sounds" (words, cries, crowing sounds, or high pitched wheeze-like sounds) can be made since these all result from air passing through the vocal cords—which in such cases is no longer possible. No "hissing" or breath sounds can be made since no air can be moved in or out of the lungs.

A partial Obstruction does not block the trachea completely—therefore, the victim will still be able to cough and make sounds. A high pitched throaty, breathy sound sometimes described as a "crowing sound" is common. The victim of a partial obstruction will "choke". They will make forceful throat-clearing noises (grunting) and forceful coughing sounds as they attempt to clear the object. Do not interfere as long as breathing continues. The victim may be able to clear the airway without help.

But if the coughing is weak and ineffective, or if the victim becomes weak or shows signs of cyanosis (a greyish blue tinge to the lips and under the fingernails), treat this partial obstruction as if it were a complete obstruction.

Airway Obstruction: Signs and Symptoms in a Conscious Adult or Child Victim.

Whether the obstruction is partial or complete, victims of an airway obstruction will suddenly appear extremely distressed. They will become anxious and animated in their attempts to breathe. Depending upon whether the obstruction is partial or complete, they will cough or make gutteral sounds as they attempt to clear the object. As they breathe they may make high pitched whistling noises. If fully obstructed they will not be able to make any breath sounds or cough.

Usually, they will either jump up and stand in a crouched position or they will remain sitting but move to a forward-leaning position.

Collateral muscles in the face and neck, not used in normal breathing, will be moving as the victim fights to clear the object and get air.

Either instinctively or by training they will make the *universal choking signal* by clutching at their throat with one or both hands.

At first they will become red in the face from their effort to breath. This is soon replaced by pallor or a greyish or bluish color indicating a lack of oxygen in the blood. If the victim is passing enough air around a partial obstruction he will remain conscious. If he is not, shortly after the obstruction occurred he will collapse, become unconscious, and finally go into cardiac arrest.

Each year some victims of an airway obstruction

die needlessly due to "social embarrassment". When they start choking, afraid of coughing-up or vomiting, they leave a crowded restaurant for the privacy of the restrooms. Often they are found there dead, and investigation shows that someone in the restaurant (staff or customer) was trained in removing an airway obstruction.

Never let a choking victim (or anyone in any distress) go to a restroom or other location where they are alone and can progress into cardiac arrest unnoticed. Anyone in any acute physical trouble should be accompanied and monitored.

Relieving a Foreign Object Obstruction in a Conscious Adult or Child

If you witness, or are summoned to someone who is choking, you need to rapidly assess if they are passing enough air. Look at the victim.

Ask "Are you choking?" Determine if the victim can talk. Even a labored word or two indicates the successful passage of air. Determine if the victim has a meaningful cough and evaluate, even with distress, whether or not the victim appears to be moving a significant amount of air.

If the victim has a partial obstruction but "good air exchange" (as witnessed by forceful coughing or good air movement even with wheezing between coughs) encourage the victim to continue spontaneous coughing and breathing efforts. Explain that you are trained, calm the victim, monitor their efforts, and have someone call for the ambulance. Do not interfere through attempts *on your part* to help clear the object.

If the victim has a partial obstruction with "poor air exchange"—as indicated by a weak ineffective cough, high pitched sound (stridor) when inhaling, increased respiratory effort, increased respiratory difficulty, and possibly an ashen or cyanotic (bluish) color—you should treat them as if they had a complete airway obstruction.

One situation in children represents an exception to these guidelines. This procedure should be initiated in a conscious child only if the airway obstruction is a witnessed or strongly suspected aspiration. If the obstruction is caused by airway swelling due to an infection such as epiglottitis or croup, these procedures may be harmful. Instead, immediately summon the emergency ambulance and maintain the child in the position of maximum comfort. The child needs advanced care as rapidly as possible.

If an adult or child has a foreign body airway obstruction:

1. Ask victim "Are you choking?" Listen and evaluate degree of distress.

If the victim has "good air exchange", encourage coughing, breathing, and clearing attempts and continue to monitor—but do *not* commence any attempts to clear the obstruction yourself.

2. If the victim has "poor air exchange" or a fully obstructed airway, go on to the Heimlich maneuver. Move so that you are standing behind the victim (who may be sitting or standing). Rapidly explain to the victim that you are trained and what you are going to do.

3. From behind, locate the victim's navel. Make a fist with one hand and place the thumb side against the victim's abdomen, in the midline slightly above the navel and well below the tip of the Xiphoid.

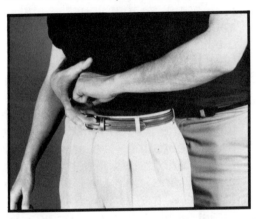

4. Grasp the part of the fist facing forward (edge with "little finger") firmly with your other hand. Your arms now fully encircle the victim's abdomen, with the fist (thumb side) placed just above the victim's navel and held in your other hand.

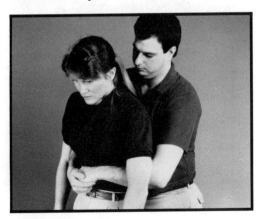

Move so that your body (or one hip) is against the back of the victim's body and stand with your feet apart, braced to keep the victim from falling if he collapses.

5. Rapidly pull forcefully and evenly with both arms, so that your fist and arms press into the victim's abdomen—producing a quick inward and upward thrust (Subdiaphragmatic thrust).

6. Relax your arms, letting them return to their original position without changing the placement of your fist and other hand from the midline position just above the navel.

7. Keep repeating the inward and upward abdominal thrust. Each thrust should be distinct and delivered with enough force to relieve the airway obstruction. Repeat thrust until either the foreign body is expelled, *or* until the victim becomes unconscious. Once you have initiated thrusts, call out for help and have someone call for the ambulance.

8. If the victim becomes unconscious or unable to stand, lower the victim to the ground
carefully and position him on his back.

Because you were present and already attempting to
clear the obstruction when the victim became unconscious, you do NOT have to perform the usual first
steps in the Obstructed Airway sequence for unconscious adults and children (such as checking for responsiveness). Instead, once the victim is laying flat
on his back:

1. Open mouth with tongue-jaw lift and
   —*in an adult,* sweep the mouth
   —*in a child,* look into the mouth and remove the object if visualized
2. Open airway with head tilt/chin lift
3. Pinch nostrils, seal mouth over victim's,
   and attempt to ventilate

Then straddle or kneel next to the victim's thighs, and
deliver abdominal thrusts. Continue "Unconscious"
steps as previously outlined until the obstruction is
cleared or the EMT's arrive and are ready to take
over.

Victim Who Is Too Large, Too Obese, or Pregnant

If the victim is too obese for you to encircle their
abdomen with reasonable ease, you will have to use
chest thrusts instead of abdominal thrusts. If the patient is pregnant, abdominal thrusts are dangerous
and chest thrusts should be used. Chest thrusts can
be performed from behind a standing or sitting patient, using the same fist and hand-over-fist method
as abdominal thrusts but with the fist positioned in

the midline of the mid-sternum, as show. Thrusts at the mid-sternum are produced with an inward pull—straight back towards the rescuer's chest.

If a victim is too tall for thrusts to be done from behind the standing victim, either sit the victim in a sturdy chair or place him on his back on the ground and use the abdominal thrust method.

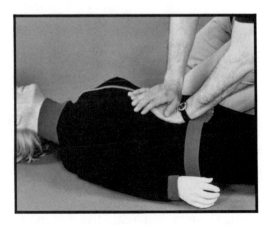

Foreign Object Airway Obstruction: Conscious Adult or Child Summary

1. Ask victim, "Are you choking?" Listen, observe victim, and assess air exchange. If "good air exchange", monitor the patient but do *NOT* intervene.
2. If "poor air exchange", or total obstruction, move so that you are behind the standing or sitting victim.
3. Make a fist with one hand and place the thumb side against the midline of the abdomen just above the navel and well below the xiphoid.
4. Grasp your fist with other hand.
5. Pull forcefully with both arms, producing a thrust inward and upward.
6. Relax your arms but do not remove them from around the victim—keep your hands just above the navel.
7. Repeat these thrusts until the foreign object is expelled or the victim becomes unconscious.

Summary, If Victim Becomes Unconscious While You Are Doing Thrusts

If the victim becomes unconscious (or can no longer stand):

8. Lower the victim to the ground so he is lying on his back on a firm hard surface.

Since you know he has an obstructed airway and is unconscious, enter the "Unconscious Obstructed" sequence at:

9. Do tongue-jaw lift and
   —In an adult, sweep the mouth.
   —In a child, look into the mouth, and remove the object if visualized.
10. Open airway with head tilt/chin lift.
11. Attempt to ventilate.

If you cannot ventilate:

12. Move next to or straddle the victim's thighs.
13. Place hands correctly on abdomen.
14. Perform 6 to 10 abdominal thrusts.
15. Repeat steps 9 thru 14 until the object is cleared or the EMT's arrive and are ready to take over.

Whichever Heimlich Maneuver is used—abdominal thrusts from behind, from the front facing the lying patient, or at the chest in obese or pregnant victims—each increases intra-thoracic pressure (air pressure in the chest). This creates an artificial cough that forces air and hopefully the foreign object to be blown out of the airway, thus relieving the obstruction.

Obstructed Airway: Conscious Infant

The Obstructed Airway procedure for a conscious infant should only be initiated if the airway obstruction is due to a witnessed aspiration or is clearly evident from the sounds and evidence of the scene, *and* if respiratory difficulty is increasing and the cough becomes ineffective. If the obstruction is caused by airway swelling due to an infection such as epiglottitis or croup, these procedures may be harmful. Instead, immediately summon the emergency ambulance and maintain the child in the position that affords the easiest breathing and most comfort.

If, in a conscious infant, airway obstruction is caused by aspiration of a foreign object:

1. Evaluate. Observe breathing difficulty, and if "poor air exchange" exists or respiratory difficulty is increasing and the cough is ineffective, or if full airway obstruction is present (no air exchange, no crying, etc.) If these are seen, continue with the following steps:

2. Sandwich the infant between your arms and turn him over, supporting the head and neck so that the infant is face down on your forearm. The infant's legs should straddle your upper arm with the head and neck supported by your hand and with the head lower than the trunk.

3. Support your forearm on your thigh or

other firm object and deliver four back blows forcefully between the shoulder blades with the heel of your other hand.

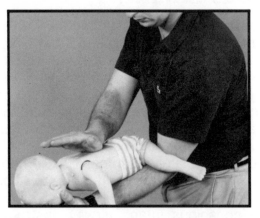

4. While supporting the infant's head, sandwich him between your arms and turn him over. The infant should be face up and supported on your forearm, with his head supported by your hand and lower than his trunk.
5. Support your forearm on your thigh or other firm surface and deliver four thrusts

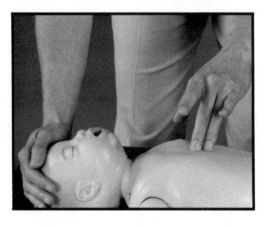

in the midsternal region in the same manner as chest compressions, but at a slower rate.

6. Repeat steps 2 thru 5 until either the foreign body is expelled or the infant becomes unconscious. As soon as you begin this sequence, call out for "Help!" and have someone call for the ambulance. It is important to carefully monitor the infant's consciousness—and to switch to the "Unconscious" procedure as soon as unconsciousness is noted.

If the infant becomes unconscious—since you know it is a foreign body obstruction, and already are in the process of treating, and have determined unresponsiveness—you enter the "Unconscious Infant Obstructed Airway" sequence at:

7. Do tongue-jaw lift, look in mouth, and remove foreign body if visualized.
8. Open airway with head tilt/chin lift.
9. Seal your mouth over the infant's mouth and nose and attempt to ventilate.
10. Supporting his head and neck, turn the infant face down over your supported forearm, with his head lower than his trunk.
11. Deliver four back blows forcefully between the shoulder blades with the heel of your other hand.
12. Supporting the infant's head and neck, turn him on his back with his head lower than his trunk.
13. Deliver four thrusts in the midsternal region in the same manner as external chest compressions, but at a slower rate.
14. Repeat steps 7 thru 13 until successful or

the EMT's arrive and are ready to take over.

Foreign Body Obstruction in Conscious Infant Summary

(Remember: if obstruction is caused by airway swelling due to infection, these procedures may be harmful).

Upon witnessed or suspected foreign body aspiration:

1. Observe for "poor air exchange" or complete obstruction.
2. Supporting head and neck with one hand, straddle the infant over your forearm and support your forearm with head lower than trunk.
3. Deliver four back blows forcefully between shoulder blades with the heel of your other hand.
4. While supporting the head, sandwich the infant between your forearms and turn him on back with head lower than trunk.
5. Deliver four chest thrusts in midsternal region (same as chest compressions, but slower).
6. Repeat steps 2 thru 5 until the object is expelled or the infant becomes unconscious.

Summary If Conscious Obstructed Infant Becomes Unconscious

If a conscious infant with a foreign body obstruction becomes unconscious:

7. Do tongue-jaw lift, remove object if visualized.
8. Open airway with head tilt/chin lift.
9. Seal your mouth over infant's mouth and nose, attempt to ventilate.
10. Supporting head and neck, turn infant face down and support him on your forearm with head lower than trunk.
11. Deliver four back blows between the infant's shoulders with the heel of your other hand.
12. Supporting head and neck, turn infant face up and support him on your forearm with head lower than trunk.
13. Deliver four chest thrusts in the mid-sternum.
14. Repeat steps 7 thru 13 until successful or the EMT's arrive and are ready to take over.

Special Situations in Giving Basic Life Support

Drowning

When a near drowning occurs, artificial ventilation or CPR must be started as quickly as possible. However, because of the special circumstances, you should be aware of several complications associated with drowning.

First, do not attempt a water rescue unless you are trained to do so. Again: don't become the next victim. Work from a boat or other flotation device. Do not attempt a swimming rescue unless you are trained to do so.

Second, do not give chest compressions in the water as they will be ineffective. (Remember, the victim must be on his back on a hard, firm surface.) Instead, get the arrested victim out of the water as fast as you can. However, mouth-to-mouth ventilation can and should be given in the water. As soon as you can stand, start mouth-to-mouth breathing and continue to move out of the water.

In a shallow water diving accident, the victim is very likely to have a neck injury which could lead to paralysis. Therefore, you must attempt to keep the victim on his or her back in the water, with the head and neck in a neutral position—that is, not bent forward, back, or to the side. If you do give mouth-to-mouth, use the modified jaw thrust method. Do not try to haul the victim of a shallow water diving accident out of the pool; when the EMT's arrive they will have backboards and will be able to slide a board under the victim and lift him from the water with minimal danger of further neck injury. Of course, if the victim is in cardiac arrest you will have to get him or her out of the water first in order to start CPR.

Another point to remember is that many drowning victims have either inhaled water into the lungs or swallowed a good deal, or both. Use the Heimlich maneuver—either chest or abdominal thrusts—before CPR to increase the chances of good ventilation. If possible, use the Heimlich maneuver with the victim's head lower than his torso.

And last, every near drowning victim—even if they were only underwater for a short time or didn't need resuscitations or were resuscitated but appear all right—should be taken to the hospital. Aspiration of even a small amount of water can result in an aspiration pneumonia. Immediate medical care can provide treatment to avoid a developing infection.

Cold Water Near Drowning

Victims who have been submerged in cold water for an extended period—*even up to an hour or more*—can be resuscitated even though they may seem dead. The victim's skin will be bluish, pulse and respiration may be so shallow and infrequent as to be undetectable. Logic may tell you that after so long a time underwater, the victim must be dead. But it is crucial that you do not give up on such a victim. When a person falls suddenly into very cold water, the body exhibits a defense reaction called the "mammalian diving reflex." The metabolic rate is reduced as a result of immersion hypothermia, and breathing and circulation slow—cutting the body's need for oxygen. Thus, it is possible for a victim of cold-water near drowning to be revived even after being submerged for what may seem to be a hopelessly long time. You should begin CPR immediately, but do not attempt to warm the victim. This should be done in the hospital.

Electric Shock

Electric shock can produce cardiac arrest. What makes this a special situation is the hazard involved. Before you make any attempt to help the victim, you must be certain that you are not in any danger. The power must be turned off at the source—this includes downed power lines. Only then it is safe to drag the victim away from the power source and begin CPR. The best thing you can do is to get professional help fast.

In a private residence, pulling the house master switch "off," only assures the current is off, if you are sure it is not a sub-master or that no other master box exists. Having more than one "box" is common where an old house has been remodelled or an addition has been added.

Outdoor wires are live until they are confirmed as disconnected at a transformer pole. Live wires may spark and "dance" or they may *not* do anything. Guessing at it, or "thinking" an item will act as an insulator is how rescuers get killed. All outdoor wires must be considered to be live and have high voltage.

Don't go near the victim until the power company or firefighters say it is safe.

One More Key Point About Basic Life Support

This chapter has dealt with the various elements of basic life support:

- Assessing the problem
- Airway management
- Artificial ventilation (mouth-to-mouth rescue breathing)
- Special situations
- Cardiopulmonary Rescusitation—CPR
- Clearing a foreign body airway obstruction in a conscious victim
- Clearing a foreign body airway obstruction in an unconscious victim

These represent a variety of steps and skills that you need to learn for adult, child, and infant victims. Once you understand these steps you will need to review and study the Summary pages for each skill to learn the different sequences.

You should not attempt to use these skills after only reading this book.

Basic Life Support skills must be practiced in hands-on sessions on a CPR mannequin and under the supervision of a qualified BLS instructor in a course that meets the American Heart Association's standards.

Chapter 3
Common Emergencies: Trauma

Emergencies fall into two categories: *trauma* and *medical emergencies.* These terms describe the origin of the problem. *Trauma* is a physical injury or wound caused by external force or violence. A *medical emergency* is a condition resulting from a problem within the body.

Both trauma and medical emergencies run the gamut from minor to life threatening: from a scraped knee to severe bleeding; from indigestion to heart attack. Here we will concentrate only on the very serious or life-threatening situations, when the problem is beyond your ability to treat, and help is needed right away. Remember that the definition of an emergency is not always clear-cut. If you *think* it is an emergency, treat it as one.

Shock

Because of the seriousness of shock, it is perhaps the best place to begin any discussion of trauma. Shock is the failure of the cardiovascular system to provide sufficient oxygenated blood to the tissues and organs of the body. It can result from many different injuries or diseases. When oxygenated blood flow drops below minimum levels, or stops, organs begin to suffocate and die.

Shock may contribute to the severity of *any* injury or sudden illness. It is extremely dangerous to the patient—especially because it is often overlooked. When untreated, shock can become progressively worse, eventually reaching an irreversible stage resulting in death.

There are two causes of shock:

1. *A malfunction of the heart or blood vessels.*

   When the sick or injured heart loses the ability to pump adequate amounts of blood, the circulation of necessary oxygen and nutrients to the cells and tissues and organs is reduced, and shock is the result.

   Blood vessels, which dilate or constrict to regulate the blood pressure and amount of blood flowing to a particular organ or tissue, can also lose their ability to function. This can cause a drastic drop in blood pressure and again, shock results.

2. *Fluid loss.*

   Fluid loss usually means blood loss as a result of bleeding— internal or external. However, it can also be caused by severe, prolonged diarrhea and vomiting or profuse sweating without fluid replacement. Burn victims may lose *plasma* (the clear liquid part of the blood), sending them into shock.

   Whatever the cause, when there is insufficient fluid volume there will be insufficient blood flow to provide the amount of oxygenated blood the body needs for survival. Shock ensues. If the cause of the shock is not controlled or reversed, death may occur.

Symptoms of Shock

- If the victim is conscious, he or she will feel restless or anxious.
- The skin will be pale, cold, and clammy. As shock progresses, the skin may take on a greyish or bluish tinge—the condition called cyanosis—from lack of oxygen in the blood.
- The pulse will be rapid and weak, since the heart—in an effort to increase circulation—pumps faster. If the heart is weakened, or the blood or fluid loss continues, there is a continuing downward spiral.
- The victim will pant as the body tries to get more air.
- The victim may be thirsty.
- The victim may be nauseated, and may vomit.
- As shock increases the victim will have reduced levels of consciousness, finally becoming unconscious and unresponsive.

What to Do

1. First you must stop any bleeding, then follow these steps:
2. Keep the patient lying down and quiet. If the injuries permit, raise the patient's feet about eighteen inches to improve the flow of blood to the vital organs (brain, heart, liver, lungs, etc.)
3. Cover the patient with a blanket to retain body heat.
4. Do not give the patient anything to

drink, even though he or she may be thirsty. The exception to this rule is when shock is caused by prolonged diarrhea or vomiting. Under these circumstances, give water in small sips.

5. Watch the patient continuously and monitor the airway and breathing until help takes over. Shock can cause the person's condition to deteriorate rapidly. All victims of trauma should be treated for shock.

Bleeding

Severe bleeding, internal or external, can be rapidly fatal. You must control severe external bleeding to minimize further blood loss and to prevent shock.

What to Do

Bleeding is controlled by direct pressure—applying enough pressure to the wound to slow or stop the bleeding. Simply place your hand over the wound and press. If you have a clean handkerchief you can place it over the wound before applying direct pressure. However, you should not waste time looking for one. Do not use a bath towel or any thick cloth or layers of cloth, as these will not transmit the direct pressure to the blood vessel and bleeding will not be controlled. Direct pressure should be applied immediately, and should be maintained until help arrives and takes over.

If the bleeding is from an arm or leg, you should elevate it while you apply direct pressure. Do not, however, elevate a limb that is, or might be, fractured. If the victim is alert, it is possible to have him or her apply the pressure. If the victim is bleeding from more than one place, attempt to control the most severe bleeding first.

There are some circumstances when direct pressure must be applied in a special way: a nosebleed, for example, can usually be controlled by pinching the nostrils just below the bony part.

If there is an object in the wound it *should not* be removed. It may be blocking several vessels, preventing them from bleeding. Furthermore, it may be broken or jagged, so that its removal would cause further damage. Such objects are best removed in the hospital. To apply direct pressure under these circumstances, place your hand around the object. (It may be necessary to stabilize the object with your other hand.) In any case, be careful not to push, pull, or move the object in any way.

If the wound has been caused by a gunshot, there may be an exit wound, where the bullet came out. Bleeding at both the entrance wound and the exit wound must be controlled.

If the injury has caused parts of the abdomen to protrude, *do not apply pressure.* Simply place a damp towel or sheet over the wound.

If a part of the body has been amputated, locate the amputated part and be sure that the EMTs know where it is. (If possible, wrap it in plastic and keep it cold. *Do Not* place it in water or in contact with ice. It may be possible, under optimum conditions, for surgeons to reattach the severed part.)

In almost all cases, direct pressure will be enough to control bleeding, even from an amputation. However, if the bleeding is so severe that you cannot control it, as a last resort you may have to apply a tourniquet.

Note: You should not attempt to apply direct pressure to stop bleeding from the vagina. You can use towels or pads to absorb the blood, but nothing should be inserted into the vagina.

Applying a Tourniquet

A tourniquet should only be used when it seems probable that the victim will bleed to death before help arrives. Tourniquets are applied only to limbs, and only when you cannot control the bleeding by direct pressure. Applying a tourniquet is dangerous because it cuts off the blood not just in the damaged vessel, but in *all* the blood vessels to the affected limb. Thus, a tourniquet can result in the loss of the limb from lack of blood. A tourniquet can also severely damage nerves.

Once a tourniquet has been applied, you should note the time. Every minute the tourniquet remains on increases the chance that the limb will be lost.

In order to apply a tourniquet you will need:

- A soft, wide cloth, such as a scarf or tie. (A narrow cloth will increase the possibility of nerve damage, as will a hard one: therefore, never use a strap or belt.)
- A short stick, ruler, pen, etc.

To apply the tourniquet:

1. Wrap the cloth twice around the arm or leg and tie a half-knot. The cloth should be placed close to the wound, and above it— *between* the wound and the heart. (*Not* at the wrist or elbow.)
2. Place the stick on the half-knot and tie a square knot around it.

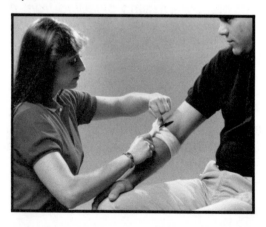

3. Twist the stick until the bleeding stops.
4. Tie the stick in place with the end of the cloth and another cloth. This is done by laying the stick flat and wrapping the cloth around it.
5. Once you have applied a tourniquet, do not remove it.

Internal Bleeding

Usually, traumatic injury is obvious—you can see the blood. But this is not always the case. A hard blow, a fall, or other accident can cause severe internal injury that may not be immediately obvious. Because internal bleeding is often difficult to recognize, the patient's condition can become critical. The external injury may appear minor, but the internal injury can be life-threatening. Therefore, any victim of a major car crash or serious fall should be seen at the hospital.

Numerous medical conditions can also cause internal bleeding—for example: ulcers, aneurysm, or cancer. Miscarriage, etopic pregnancy, and abortion may also be causes. Whatever the reason, internal bleeding is a life-threatening emergency. Although you cannot "see" internal bleeding, identify its presence by looking for signs of inadequate circulation. You can recognize inadequate circulation by *any* of the following symptoms:

- Unexplained signs of shock.
- Overly rapid (more than 100) or slow (less than 60) pulse rate.
- The vomiting of blood. ("Coffee ground" appearance).
- Blood in the bowel. ("Tarry" stool.)

- Prolonged bleeding from the vagina.
- Sudden, unexplained weakness.
- Weakness or dizziness when moved to standing from a sitting or lying position.
- Repeated fainting.
- Unexplained unconsciousness.

The preceeding list of symptoms are indicators of a substantial reduction in circulation. Circulatory insufficiency (lower than healthy level to meet the body's needs) can result from:

- *Anemia*—the lack of production of adequate components of blood.
- *Chemical imbalance*—this can result from illness or improper intake (improper diet or fluid input.)
- *Reduced cardiac output*—a reduction in the heart's pumping ability which may result from a heart attack with clear symptoms, or a heart attack which has *no* normal symptoms or cardiac pain associated with it.
- *Fluid loss*—from diarrhea, vomitting or vast urination (Vast urination can result from an overdose of "water pills").
- *Blood loss*—from sudden external or internal bleeding or chronic internal bleeding (common, for example, in ulcers or other G.I. bleeding.)

It is sometimes difficult, even in the hospital, to immediately determine which of these factors is the cause to the reduced circulation. The specific cause is not a key consideration prehospital.

Recognition of reduced circulation is key. Regardless of its cause, any circulatory problem producing any of these symptoms (or combination of them) must be considered serious and can be, or rapidly become, life threatening.

What to Do

Recognize the signs and understand that a potential cardiac problem or internal bleeding may be present.

Treat the victim for shock.

Without delay, call for the emergency ambulance. Keep the patient calm and do not let him eat or drink.

Monitor the patient and be able to provide Basic Life Support if needed.

Direct pressure is *not* effective for internal bleeding; in fact it may aggravate the problem and should *not* be considered.

Burns

Burns can be caused by heat or chemicals. Whether a burn is an emergency or not depends on the depth of the burn, how much of the body area it covers, and/or what part of the body is involved. Burns are normally classified by the amount of damage done.

First-Degree Burns

First-degree burns affect only the topmost layers of skin. They usually involve redness, mild swelling, and pain. They are best treated by bathing the burn area with cold water—or applying cold compresses, the sooner the better—for about 20 30 minutes, followed by a mild vaseline type of ointment dressing. They are uncomfortable, but they heal quickly. Generally, first-degree burns are not serious. If they involve more than a small area of skin, however, the victim should see a doctor.

Second-Degree Burns

Second-degree burns are more serious because they affect deeper layers of skin. They are also much more painful than first-degree burns. Second-degree burns will appear red or mottled, blistering will occur, there will be swelling, and the surface of the skin may appear wet. This is because plasma is being lost through the damaged skin. If much plasma is lost, the victim will go into shock.

What to Do
1. Stop the burning process.
2. Remove any jewelry (retains heat and can cut off circulation if swelling occurs.)

If a small area of an arm, hand or foot is involved:
3. Place the burned part in cold water. This will help alleviate pain.

If other:

4. First, cover the burn with a clean cloth that has been immersed in cold water. Later, the burn should be covered with a dry cloth or dry clean sheet.

There are a couple of "don'ts" when treating second-degree burns:

1. *Do not* break blisters or remove pieces of skin.
2. *Do not* use anything but water on the burn.
3. *Do Not* use an overabundance of cold water, as shock and chills may result. Apply cold cloths *only* to painful but relatively small areas—not to exceed 10% of the body surface.

Third-Degree Burns

Third-degree burns destroy all layers of skin, extending at least to the subcutaneous (under the skin) tissue. They may cause damage to muscle tissue. Sometimes the depth of the burn can extend to the bone. The burn will appear white or charred, and muscle or bone may be visible.

Any third-degree burn must be considered an emergency requiring an ambulance and transport to the hospital emergency department. Call for help.

What to Do

1. Cover the burn with a clean, dry cloth or sheet.
2. Don't attempt to remove pieces of clothing that adhere to the wound, and

don't put anything else on the burned area.

3. If burns are of the face, have the victim sit up. Watch for any difficulty in breathing. Severe facial burns may indicate that the victim has inhaled superheated air, causing burns of the respiratory tract. These burns may cause swelling severe enough to obstruct the airway. If there is trouble breathing, keep the airway open and provide artificial ventilation if needed.

Chemical Burns

Chemical burns of the skin should be treated by thoroughly rinsing and flooding the area with cold water for at least 15 minutes. The washing should be done with a hose or in a shower, and the victim's clothes should be removed. Be careful not to get any of the chemical on yourself.

If the chemical is a powder, brush away the excess powder before you begin washing. Be sure to use a cloth or a towel when brushing away the chemical; avoid coming in contact with it.

Chemical burns of the eye are particularly serious and can result in the loss of sight. The eye, eyelid, and face should be washed for at least 15 minutes in cool water. Pour water from the inner corner of the eye outward, holding the eyelid open if necessary. If only one eye is affected, be careful not to let the chemical wash into the unaffected eye. Treatment should continue until help arrives.

Chest Injuries

A chest injury can be particularly serious. Any fall, car accident, or other blunt trauma can cause ribs to be fractured. Fractured ribs can be merely painful or life threatening. When two or more ribs are fractured in two places, or the breastbone is fractured in two places, a floating rib section called a "flail" results—a serious emergency. A fractured rib may also puncture a lung.

The danger of any rib fracture is that it will cause inadequate ventilation. The signs of a chest injury will be pain and difficulty breathing.

What to Do

You should not move this patient, but monitor breathing and be prepared to give mouth-to-mouth ventilation.

Puncture Wound to the Chest

A puncture wound that breeches the chest wall will cause air to enter the chest, creating a pneumothorax—collapse of a lung— which will impair both breathing and circulation. Because you'll hear the air entering the chest, this type of wound is called a *sucking chest wound.*

What to Do

    1. Seal the wound to prevent air from entering the chest cavity. This is most

easily done by sealing the heel or palm of your hand over the wound. Another method is to place a piece of household plastic wrap (which extends 2 inches beyond the wound) over the wound and fasten it by taping the edges with adhesive tape.
2. Monitor the patient's breathing and be prepared to assist ventilation if necessary.

Eye Injuries

Eye injuries can be blunt or penetrating. Either can be very serious, requiring emergency care.

Blunt eye injury involves a blow to the eye. It can result in the eye being dislodged from its socket.

What to Do

1. Cover the uninjured eye loosely with a clean cloth.
2. If the injured eye is still in its socket, it too should be covered with the cloth. If the eye is out of the socket, place a paper cup over it and keep the patient flat on his or her back.
3. Do not touch or put any pressure on the eye.

Penetrating eye injury occurs when an object pierces the eye. Such an injury is very serious. It can easily result in blindness.

What to Do

1. Do not remove the object or put any pressure on the eye.
2. Cover both eyes loosely with a clean cloth.
3. Keep the patient calm and flat on his or her back.

Fractures

A fracture is a break or crack in a bone and can be either *closed* or *open*. *Closed* simply means that although the bone is broken, it does not protrude through the skin. An *open* fracture is one in which the bone ends have torn through the muscle and skin and may be visible.

It is not always easy to diagnose a fracture. Other injuries display similar symptoms; these include dislocations (the displacement of a bone from its attachment to another bone at a joint) and sprains and strains (muscle and tendon problems). Because the only certain way to determine the type of injury is by x-ray, you should not attempt to decide between fracture, dislocation, sprain, or strain, but treat them all as if they were fractures.

Suspect a fracture if the cause of the problem *could* have resulted in a fracture: a fall, an automobile accident, etc. Sometimes the victim will be "guarding," that is, protecting a possible fracture site. The victim may report that he or she cannot move, or may have heard or felt a snap. The victim may report pain and tenderness of the injured part. There may also be the sensation of broken bones rubbing together. Other signs of fracture: obvious deformity, pain when touched, swelling and/or discoloration, and a difference between the corresponding bones on the other side of the body.

What to Do

The goal in treating a fracture is to prevent further damage. Therefore, you want to prevent the fractured part from moving.

1. Allow the victim to maintain the fractured part in a comfortable position.
2. Stabilize the fractured part by gently supporting it with your hands.
3. With an open fracture, it may be necessary to control bleeding as well. Apply direct pressure even if it is at the fracture site. Remember, stopping serious bleeding is a high priority.
4. Continue to support the fracture until help arrives. As with any other major injury, be sure the victim is breathing normally, and treat for shock. However, *do not* elevate a fractured arm or leg.

There are three areas of the body where fractures can be particularly serious and therefore need special care. These are the head or face, spine, and chest.

Head and Face Injuries

The most important thing to remember about a head injury is that any force powerful enough to cause major injury to the head may very likely cause spinal injury as well. Therefore, all victims of head injury must be treated with extreme care. Signs of a serious head injury:

- Loss of consciousness for any length of time.
- Difficulty breathing.
- Clear or blood-tinged fluid coming from the nose or ears.
- Partial or complete paralysis.
- Pupils of unequal size.
- Speech disturbance.
- Convulsions.
- Vomiting.
- A slow and weak pulse.
- Impaired vision/sudden blindness.

The most important thing you can do for someone with a severe head injury is to be sure that he or she is breathing normally. You must provide artificial ventilation if needed and keep the airway clear of fluid and vomit.

What to Do

1. The victim should be kept calm and still in a semi-seated position.

2. *Do not* elevate the feet—this will send more blood to the head, possibly making matters worse.
3. Do not attempt to stop fluid from coming out of the nose or ears.
4. *Do not* give the victim anything to eat or drink.

For major injury to the face, mouth, and jaw, your main concern must be the victim's breathing. Such an injury may cause the airway to be blocked with blood, making breathing difficult. It may be necessary to give artificial ventilation. You may need to support the victim's head to keep the airway open.

Remember, with any major head injury, the spine may also have been injured. Therefore, try to keep the head in a neutral position: don't allow the head to bend forward or back or to the side.

Spine Injuries

Spine injuries can be very serious. The spinal cord within the spine is the main route of nerve impulses from the brain. Should the cord be injured, communication between the brain and the body below the injury will be interrupted. Paralysis will result. Therefore, any suspected spine injury must be treated carefully. Even slight movement can cause permanent damage.

The best indication as to the likelihood of a spine injury is the type of accident. For example, if the victim has suffered a severe fall or a car accident, you must assume a spine injury is present and treat accordingly. In a diving accident, the victim may have hit his or her head on the bottom of the pool or on a rock. This victim, too, must be treated as if spine injury is present. Other indications of spine injury include: pain in the neck or back, tenderness when the spine or neck is touched, pain when the victim moves, numbness or tingling in the arm or legs, and of course, paralysis. Paralysis will occur on both sides of the body below the point at which the spine is injured. If the injury is in the upper neck, it is possible that the victim's ability to breathe will be affected, and you will have to give mouth-to-mouth ventilation. In addition, the victim of a spine injury may go into shock.

What to Do

The object in treating the injured spine is to prevent movement.

1. If the victim is seated, in a car for example, the head should be supported in a neutral, upright position. The victim should not be allowed to bend forward or back or to the side. However, if there is any pain or resistance to moving the head, support it in the position you find it, provided the airway is open and the patient is breathing normally.
2. If the victim is lying down, the head should be supported in a neutral position and the victim kept flat.
3. Never move anyone who may have an injury to the neck or back. This should only be done by trained responders. Any move-

ment may aggravate the injury. Only move the patient if the scene is so unsafe that the danger to the patient outweighs the possibility of further spine injury.
4. Treat the victim for shock without elevating the legs.
5. Watch the victim's breathing, and be prepared to give mouth-to-mouth ventilation if necessary.
6. If the victim is in cardiac arrest, CPR will have to take precedence over other concerns: If necessary, you may move the patient to administer CPR.

Unconsciousness

Unconsciousness other than a simple faint is an emergency. A patient who is unconscious and cannot be aroused or who can be aroused but slides back into unconsciousness must be given immediate treatment. This is also true for anyone who loses consciousness after an accident but has recovered, or anyone who can't remember what happened just before or just after the accident. (This is often a sign that the victim was unconscious, even though he or she doesn't remember being unconscious.)

What to Do

1. In any serious accident or fall, violent movement to the spine and damage may have occurred. The victim's head should be supported and held in the

position in which it is found (whether he is sitting or lying), and the victim should **not** be moved. Some key exceptions to be noted are:

- If the victim is having difficulty breathing you may have to slowly and carefully move his head into a neutral in line position and then hold it.
- If the victim is on his back and starts to vomit, stabilize the head and neck and with the aid of others roll him onto his side as a unit. When vomiting stops, clear it, and as a unit roll him back onto his back and hold the head.

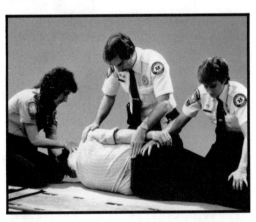

- If the scene is dangerous you will have to move him to safety. This should be done with as little movement to the spine as possible (i.e.:— dragging him by his arms rather than lifting him.)

2. If you are sure there are no injuries to the neck or spine, roll the victim onto his or her side so his head rests on his arm and the chin is pointed downward (the "coma position"). This will prevent the tongue or fluids from obstructing the airway. Once the victim is in this position, you should continue to monitor his breathing. If the patient vomits, you will have to clear all the vomit from his mouth. Use your fingers to do this.

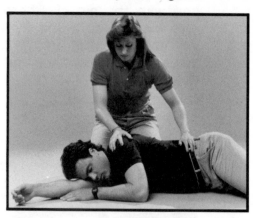

3. Never give anything by mouth to an unconscious patient or any victim of trauma.

Automobile Accidents

If you are involved in an automobile accident or stop to help at the scene, there are several points to remember.

1. Be sure the scene is safe. If there is any

danger of fire, if electrical wires are down, or if the vehicle is precariously positioned, stay away until professional help arrives.

2. Park your car a safe distance from the accident on the shoulder of the road. Turn your emergency flashers on.

3. Call or send for help. Try to get at least two people to report the accident. (Remember, the police monitor CB channel 9.) The report should include

    • accident location, including nearby cross streets, landmarks, exit numbers, or utility pole numbers.

    • type of accident: how many cars, whether there are injuries, and how many people are involved.

    • your name.

4. Enlist bystanders to warn oncoming cars, direct traffic, and control other bystanders.

5. If you decide that a victim must be moved from the car before help arrives—for example, if the victim is in cardiac arrest, or if the scene may become unsafe—you should try to protect his or her head, neck and back. This can be done as follows:

    • Put your arms around the victim under the armpits, and grasp your hands in front of the chest.

    • Turn the victim in the seat so that his or her back is facing the door.

    • Keeping the victim's head against your chest, drag the victim out of the car as gently as possible.

- Once the victim is on the ground, drag the victim away from the car. Keep the head secured, and make sure the victim remains on his or her back, in as straight a position as possible. When you are a safe distance from the car, begin treatment.

Chapter 4
Common Emergencies: Medical

Medical emergencies result from illness and problems within the body, as opposed to trauma, which is caused by injury from an external source.

Acute Abdomen

Abdominal pain may be caused by any of several conditions—from minor viral infections to the more serious problems of appendicitis and peritonitis.

Even physicians sometimes have trouble determining the exact cause of acute abdominal pain—but you don't need to determine cause. Emergency treatment is the same for all these conditions.

Of course, the primary symptom for abdominal distress is pain—either local ("It hurts right *here*") or diffuse ("It hurts all over"). The abdomen may also be tender. If it feels rigid when you touch it, you can be pretty sure that something is seriously wrong. This rigidity is caused by tense abdominal muscles—the body's way to protect the affected organs. The patient will often have a rapid pulse, and may not want to move, because of the pain. Even breathing may be painful. The patient may vomit. If there is blood in the patient's vomit or bowel movement, this is an even more acute emergency. Any prolonged or recurrent abdominal pain requires prompt medical attention.

What to Do

1. Do not give the patient anything to eat or drink. (He or she may require prompt surgery, which is best done on an empty stomach.)
2. Do not give a laxative or enema.
3. Placing an ice bag over localized pain may help minimize the pain. (It will not affect the cause of the problem, however.)
4. If the patient vomits, be sure the airway is cleared.
5. Allow the patient to rest in a comfortable position with the knees drawn up.

Allergic Reactions

Allergic reactions can be caused by many things—things you touch, or food you eat, or medications you take. They can also be caused by animal bites or stings. Usually these reactions are minor and confined to the area of contact, or in the case of something ingested, nausea and vomiting or dizziness may occur. However, there can be times when an allergic reaction can become a life-threatening emergency called anaphylactic shock. In anaphylactic shock the allergic reaction may be so severe that it causes the airway to swell, possibly obstructing it. This can happen quickly, and death can result in a very few minutes.

Those who are known reactors to stings carry their own medication.

Anyone who is allergic to a medication should be sure to tell the EMTs and the physician at the hospital.

What to Do

1. Monitor the victim's breathing. If the victim develops respiratory or cardiac arrest, give Basic Life Support.
2. If the victim is a known reactor and has medication, find it, read the instructions, and help administer it immediately.
3. Because the victim's limbs may swell, remove all watches, rings, or bracelets that may restrict circulation.

Bites and Stings

A bite or a sting constitutes a medical emergency *only* if there is a large amount of swelling or if the victim suffers or is know to suffer from anaphylactic (allergic) reaction. An animal bite should be treated like any wound.

The bite of a poisonous snake or insect can be lethal for anyone; however, people who suffer from anaphylactic reaction can be killed by a single sting from an insect or bee whose sting would barely bother another individual. The reactor's airway may swell in an allergic response to the sting, causing death by asphyxiation within minutes if not dealt with promptly.

What to Do

1. Known reactors carry medication with them. Find it, read the directions, and administer it immediately. Then proceed to the following steps. (If the victim is suffering his or her first anaphylactic reaction, there will be no medication. Remain calm and proceed to the following steps.)
2. Have the patient rest quietly. The more he or she moves around, the faster the blood will circulate, carrying venom throughout the body.
3. If the sting or bite is on the fingers or hand, remove any rings, bracelets, or watches that might affect circulation to the fingers, which swell.
4. *Do not* put ice on a snake bite.
5. Place both of your hands around the arm or leg, *above* the sting or bite, and apply pressure. The goal is to prevent the spread of venom. Maintain pressure until help arrives.
6. Monitor the victim's breathing. If the victim develops respiratory or cardiac arrest, forget the sting itself and begin Basic Life Support.
7. Try to identify the insect or snake. This will help guide treatment in the hospital.

Common Poisonous Animals

1. Arizona Scorpion

2. Spiders

   Black Widow—Black with a yellow-orange hourglass marking on its underside.
   Brown Recluse—Brown with a black fiddle shape on its back.

3. Snakes

   Rattlesnake
   Copperhead
   Cottonmouth
   Coral Snake—Small, with bright red, yellow, and black bands. The red and yellow bands are next to each other.

4. Sea Animals

   Jellyfish—Portuguese Man of War, etc.
   (Wash wound with vinegar.)
   Sea Urchin
   Cone Shell
   Spine Fish
   (Wash the wound with warm water.)
   Sea Nettle
   (Wash wound with a mixture of water and baking soda.)

Chest Pains/Heart Attack

Chest pains must always be taken very seriously, particularly in an individual over 40 years of age, since they may be an indication of heart attack.

A heart attack occurs when one of the arteries leading to the heart becomes blocked, cutting off the blood supply to the heart muscle. The part of the heart muscle fed by that artery then dies, which may significantly decrease the heart's pumping ability, or alter its rhythm, or cause cardiac arrest.

Symptoms of a heart attack are
- Severe prolonged pain behind the breastbone, which may or may not radiate to the arms, neck and jaw, or back. This pain may be described as pressure or a crushing pain by the victim.
- Profuse sweating.
- Nausea, vomiting.
- Shortness of breath.
- Anxiety; a sense of impending doom.

Not all patients experience all of these symptoms. The most important symptoms are the pain and sweating.

Chest pains may also be caused by angina. Angina is caused by a temporary narrowing of an artery to the heart, interrupting blood flow to the heart muscle, but not causing permanent damage. The symptoms of angina resemble those of a heart attack, but do not last long.

They are:
- Pain, often described as "squeezing," seldom characterized as sharp or stabbing; it may radiate into the arms, neck, jaw, or back.
- Sweating, pallor, nausea.
- Usually brought on by exertion and relieved by rest.

If the pain of an angina attack lasts for more than ten minutes, it may very well prove to be a heart attack.

What to Do

1. Known sufferers from angina carry medication with them. Administer the pill under the victim's tongue, or as prescribed by the victim's doctor. Treatment for angina and heart attack is the same. *First, call the ambulance.* Then go on to the following steps.
2. Keep the patient seated upright. This usually facilitates breathing.
3. Monitor the patient's breathing.
4. Do not give the victim anything to eat or drink. Nausea and vomiting often occur during heart attacks and angina; it is better not to put anything into the stomach that the victim could regurgitate and perhaps aspirate into the lungs.
5. Be prepared to perform CPR.

Childbirth

As any healthy pregnant woman will tell you, childbirth is not an illness. It is a biological process—one with a delightful outcome. It is, however, a period of risk. Therefore, if you are in a situation where you must assist the delivery of a child, there are some instructions that will help this natural process to proceed with the minimum of difficulty.

First you need some basic information. Ask the patient: "Is this your first baby?" (As a rule, first babies take longer to deliver than subsequent babies.) "How far apart are the contractions?" (If contractions are five minutes or more apart, chances are very good that the ambulance will arrive before the child is born. If they are less than two minutes apart, birth may be imminent.) Other symptoms of imminent birth include a broken bag of waters, which may be indicated by a gush of fluid or by an ongoing trickle from the vagina; or a bloody discharge—a quantity of mucus, either bright red or brown.

What to Do

1. Have the patient lie on her back or side, whichever is more comfortable.
2. Have her remove her underwear. It is better to do this now than to wait until the last minute.
3. Have her take deep breaths. If she has been taking classes in natural childbirth,

she may have her own preferred rhythm; encourage her to make use of whatever techniques she has been given. Not only can this ease the pain of a contraction, it will give her something else to think about, and help to diminish her awareness of pain.

4. When the woman feels a strong urge to push, or to bear down, or to move her bowels, the baby is about to be born. Have her lie on her back with her knees bent.

5. Place clean towels under her buttocks. Have more clean towels ready.

6. If, during a contraction, you can see the top of the baby's head (called *crowning*), the birth is likely within the next few minutes. Encourage the mother to push with each contraction, but to rest between contractions. There is no point in pushing when no contraction is taking place.

7. As the baby's head delivers, cradle it in your hand. Don't push or pull on the infant; let the birth take place naturally.

8. There will be water and blood with the delivery. This is normal. When the baby is delivered, wipe any mucus or fluid out of its mouth with a clean washcloth.

9. Do not cut or pull on the cord. The mother will deliver the placenta in a few minutes, with contractions, just as she delivered the baby.

10. Wrap the infant in clean towels and place it on the mother's abdomen.
11. If the infant does not begin to breathe by itself, try to stimulate breathing by rubbing its back or gently slapping the soles of its feet.
12. If the baby still does not begin to breathe, provide artificial ventilation and/or CPR as needed.
13. When the mother delivers the placenta, usually within 10–20 minutes, wrap it and save it for the doctor, who will need to examine it to make sure that the entire placenta has been delivered and that no portions of it remain in the uterus.
14. Keep the placenta level with or slightly above the baby. This will help the blood to drain from the placenta to the child.

Complications

If the infant's arms or feet appear instead of its head, or when the umbilical cord can be seen in the birth canal, these are signs something is wrong. Tell the mother *not to push.*

The urge to push will be very strong, and may seem uncontrollable. When this urge comes on, tell the mother to blow hard over and over. While she is puffing in this way, she will be unable to push with full force.

Convulsions/Seizures

Convulsions are generally symptoms of some other form of illness or injury. They may be caused by a high fever, a blow to the head, acute infectious disease, or epilepsy.

A person who is having convulsions loses consciousness. The eyes roll back in the head; the muscles jerk and twitch; the jaw may be clenched, and there may be foamy saliva at the mouth. Be aware that there may be a brief period of respiratory arrest. Make sure there is a pulse present. If not, perform CPR.

What to Do

1. There is nothing you can do to stop or shorten the seizure. It will stop by itself after a few minutes. Your concern during the seizure should be to make sure that the person doesn't do self-harm.
2. Do not attempt to restrain the patient. You may hurt the patient, or be hurt yourself. (Persons in convulsions sometimes flail their arms and legs wildly; an accidental kick can be very painful.) Instead, clear the area around the patient. Remove or pad any tables or chairs that might cause injury; take away any glass objects that might break.

3. *Don't try to put anything into the patient's mouth.* There is a common misconception that a person in convulsions is in danger of swallowing his or her tongue. This is untrue, and efforts to prevent it by forcing something between the patient's teeth may only make matters worse by causing obstruction of the airway.
4. When the convulsion ends, the person may remain unconscious for a few minutes. The skin may be cool, clammy, and bluish in color. The pulse may be very shallow, and breathing may seem to be almost nonexistent. This is all normal for a recovering victim of a seizure. Place the victim on his or her side in case of vomiting. Monitor breathing, and if the victim goes into respiratory arrest, be prepared to provide ventilations.

Diabetic Coma and Insulin Shock

Diabetes mellitus is a common medical problem caused when the body produces too little insulin or no insulin at all. Insulin is essential for the metabolism of sugar. The result of this condition is a low absorption of sugar by the body cells and consequently a high level of sugar in the blood. Generally, this is a diagnosed condition that is kept under control by daily doses of insulin. There are, however, two acute emergencies that can occur. If you encounter a person exhibiting any of the signs described below, look for a bracelet that identifies him or her as a diabetic.

Diabetic Coma

This condition is usually caused when a diabetic has not taken insulin on schedule. It can also result from not eating properly, or being ill. A diabetic suffering from diabetic coma will exhibit the following symptoms:

- Strong breath odor—like nail polish remover.
- Flushed face.
- Red lips.
- Dry skin.
- Rapid breathing or hyperventilation.
- May appear confused or disoriented, or appear "drunk."
- Unconsciousness.

This patient needs immediate medical attention.

Insulin Shock (Hypoglycemia)

This condition is exactly the opposite of diabetic coma. It results from too little sugar in the blood. It can be caused by taking too much insulin or by not eating enough food. The patient will exhibit the following symptoms:

- Pale skin color.
- Moist, clammy skin.
- Rapid pulse.
- Slow and shallow breathing.
- Unconsciousness.
- Possibly convulsions.

What to do

Although these conditions are opposite, your treatment is basically the same. You should treat for shock, and if the patient is conscious, give sugar, preferably orange juice or soda—but not a diet drink, since the drink must contain sugar. The rationale is that if the victim is in insulin shock the sugar is needed, but if the victim is in diabetic coma, the small amount of sugar you give will do no harm.

In either case the ambulance must be called prior to any treatment. If the patient is unconscious, you should treat as you would any unconscious patient.

Difficulty Breathing

Difficulty breathing can result from a variety of causes. Although the treatment is the same regardless of the case, it is important to recognize the conditions that are emergencies. In all cases, the ambulance should be called immediately.

Smoke Inhalation

Smoke inhalation can cause damage to the upper and lower airway, producing swelling and impeding ventilation. It can even damage the alveoli in the lungs, producing pulmonary edema. Although pulmonary edema may not develop initially, these patients must be watched carefully, as it may develop 6–48 hours later.

The general signs of smoke inhalation are shortness of breath, coughing, difficulty in swallowing due to irritation, soot- flecked sputum, and cyanosis. The possibility of carbon monoxide poisoning associated with smoke inhalation should not be overlooked. What is true of smoke inhalation is also true of other toxic inhalants such as ammonia, nitrous oxide, sulfur dioxide, and phosgene. The victim must be removed from the toxic environment prior to treatment. You should not enter the toxic environment.

Carbon Monoxide Poisoning

Carbon monoxide (CO) poisoning occurs when carbon monoxide, a colorless, odorless, tasteless gas produced by incomplete combustion, is inhaled. CO combines with the hemoglobin in red blood cells, taking the place of oxygen and significantly reducing the amount of oxygen in the blood. A severe lack of oxygen will lead to tissue damage, unconsciousness, respiratory arrest and death. *Contrary to popular belief, "Cherry" red skin coloring is not usually seen in CO poisoning victims who are still alive.*

Any victim who has been removed from an enclosed space with an operating automobile engine or furnace should be suspected of having carbon monoxide poisoning. Remove the patient from the toxic environment and get emergency help as soon as possible. Any victim of a fire who was exposed to smoke or byproducts of burning in an enclosed space (a room), should be suspected of having CO poisoning and should have medical attention.

Pulmonary Embolism

Pulmonary embolism is a clot that has formed in the veins and has traveled through the heart into the lungs. The clot is eventually trapped in one of the smaller veins of a lung, reducing or stopping the blood supply to that portion of the lung, and causing cells to die.

Patients likely to suffer pulmonary embolism are those who have congestive heart failure (CHF); those who have had a recent heart attack or surgery; anyone with Thrombophlebitis (blood clots in veins of the leg); and those who have been bedridden for extended periods.

The signs of pulmonary embolism vary. There may be sharp pain, coughing of bloody sputum, shortness of breath, and wheezing.

Asthma, emphysema, and pulmonary edema, the next conditions discussed, are usually chronic conditions that are kept in check by medication. They become emergencies when the patient suffers from a severe attack that is not controlled by the prescribed medication.

Asthma

Asthma is a common disease at any age, although onset below 2 years of age or over 60 is rare. Approximately half of all asthmatic patients are allergic to one of more substances—common offenders being pollens, molds, spores, animal hair, feathers, dust, etc. Attacks may be triggered by a respiratory infection, cold, flu, or pneumonia.

In an acute asthmatic attack, the muscles of the

airway contract, narrowing the passage. The lining of the airway becomes swollen, causing further narrowing. Finally, the swollen lining begins to secrete a thick mucus, which acts to plug the already narrowed airway. This results in a decrease of oxygen getting into the blood.

The patient will feel "tightness" in the chest and progressive anxiety. The rate and effort of breathing increase. You will hear a high-pitched sound when the victim exhales. The victim may eventually become exhausted from the labor of breathing. At this point he or she will become increasingly pale and sweaty, and respiratory arrest may occur.

Emphysema/COPD

Emphysema (Chronic Obstructive Pulmonary Disease) results from long-term, progressive destruction of the alveoli in the lungs. It may be caused by many years of asthma, chronic bronchitis, heavy smoking, or heavy dust inhalation. The patient suffering from emphysema will exhibit the same symptoms as the asthma patient.

Pulmonary Edema/CHF

Pulmonary Edema (Congestive Heart Failure, CHF) results from an increase of pressure in the blood vessels in the lungs. This is turn causes fluid to ooze out of the small blood vessels (capillaries) into the lung tissue, filling the lungs. The patient has great difficulty breathing, and may have the feeling of suffocation. In fact, without treatment, the patient will drown in body fluid.

There are many causes of pulmonary edema. The most common is left heart failure, as in hypertensive disease or heart attack (acute myocardialinfarction). Direct damage to the lung can also cause pulmonary edema. Other causes include smoke inhalation (or other toxic inhalation), near-drowning, aspiration, pneumonia, narcotic overdose, and high-altitude pulmonary edema.

Whatever the cause, pulmonary edema is a serious emergency because it limits the patient's ability to breathe and can result in respiratory arrest. Advanced signs include frothy and blood- tinged sputum and distended neck veins. The patient will insist upon sitting upright and will lean slightly forward, in an effort to take in as much air as possible. The ventilatory rate will be rapid and shallow.

What to Do for All Patients with Any of the Above Breathing Difficulties

1. Have the patient sit up for greater ease in breathing.
2. If difficulty continues for a prolonged period, the victim will become exhausted from the effort and may go into respiratory arrest. Be prepared to assist with mouth-to-mouth ventilation.
3. For patients suffering from asthma, emphysema, and pulmonary edema, you may assist in administering prescribed medications. However, do not neglect to call the ambulance.

Hyperventilation

Hyperventilation syndrome can be a response to anxiety or to a medical problem. The patient breathes rapidly beyond control in an effort to get as much air as possible, feeling he or she is not getting enough.

Patients will report numbness and tingling of the extremities and lips. As the syndrome continues, patients may develop cramping of the hands and feet. All this is the result of an unusually low level of carbon dioxide in the blood. Treatment should be directed at rebalancing the carbon dioxide level. Often this is done by having the patient breathe into a paper bag, rebreathing his or her own carbon dioxide. This, however, can be extremely dangerous unless you are sure that the hyperventilation is not a result of a condition such as diabetic coma.

Difficulty Breathing: Children

Epiglottitis

Epiglottitis is an acute respiratory disease caused by infection of the epiglottis, which swells up, becomes bright red, and can entirely obstruct the trachea. The patient may be any age, but is usually a child over 4 years old. The patient is usually sick for roughly 8 hours before airway symptoms become evident. Symptoms include high fever and high-pitched breathing (stridor)—indicating that the airway is narrowing. The patient has difficulty speaking and swallowing, drools saliva, sits upright to make breathing easier, and is anxious. It is urgent that this patient get to the hospital.

What to Do

1. Do not try to ease breathing by attempts to open the airway. This can be lethal, as it can set off the patient's gag reflex. In turn, this will cause the swollen epiglottis to close over the trachea—resulting in respiratory arrest.
2. *Do Not* put anything into the patient's mouth or throat. *Do Not* attempt to visualize or examine the back of the throat.
3. Keep the patient in an upright, seated position.

Croup

Croup is also an acute respiratory disease found most frequently in children below the age of 4 years. It is caused by an infection that involves the tissues of the larynx, especially the vocal cords. It does not involve the epiglottis, and the patient has no difficulty swallowing. It usually occurs several days after the onset of a cold or other infection. There is usually a low or moderate fever and, as the laryngeal edema increases, a progressive "hard" cough which sounds like the bark of a seal. It occurs mostly at night.

What to Do

1. Call the doctor.
2. Turn on the hot water in the shower, and allow the bathroom to fill with steam.
3. Hold the child in a seated position in the steam-filled room. This may help ease breathing.
4. Monitor breathing.

Drug Overdose

People may suffer from an overdose of prescription drugs or narcotics, accidentally or on purpose. Any type of drug overdose is like a poisoning—the victim has put something into his or her body that causes the body to react adversely.

Symptoms of drug overdose may vary, depending on the drug taken. The victim may become incoherent, sleepy and hard to arouse, or overexcited, angry, and uncontrollable. The narcotic victim's pupils may contract to pinpoints. Habitual drug abusers may show needle-marks on their arms.

What to Do

1. Try to find the *container* the prescription drug came in. The name of the substance should be on the label. EMTs will need this information and will pass it on to the physician at the hospital.
2. If the patient is conscious, monitor breathing, and try to keep the patient calm.
3. If the patient is hallucinating and frightened, offer sympathy and understanding. You may be able to calm the patient.
4. If the victim becomes physically violent, *leave.* EMTs are trained to deal with this type of situation; let them handle it. If you try to deal with it yourself, you may get hurt.

Emotional Problems

People may suffer from varying degrees of emotional instability, ranging from maladjustments that come and go and are easily handled, through neuroses—problems that can sometimes keep the person from functioning normally and relating to others, but that don't prevent a person from getting by in society—to psychosis—serious mental impairment that prevents normal participation in society and may require hospitalization.

Neurotics may suffer from anxiety, or phobia—fear of a particular situation, such as heights or darkness or, perhaps, dogs. Prolonged depression may be expressed by apathy, pessimism, and a feeling of always being too tired to do anything.

Psychosis may be physical in origin (alcoholism, hardening of the arteries, certain diseases, and brain injury can all cause psychosis), or nonorganic (such as paranoia, schizophrenia, or manic depressive psychosis—recently renamed Bipolar Disease).

What to Do

In general, victims of neuroses and psychoses need help from trained people. Try to reach the person's doctor. Don't argue with the person, and never imply that you think he or she is mentally disturbed—this might only arouse anger. Be kind, reassuring, and firm.

If the patient is about to harm himself or herself or someone else, offer a diversion. Do not try to restrain the patient. If he or she becomes violent, remember that your own safety must take precedence, and leave.

Frostbite

When frostbite occurs, ice crystals form in the tissues of the body. The victim's skin will be cold, hard, white, and numb. There may also be blisters. The affected parts will of course feel intensely cold; however, there may not be any pain, and the victim may not know that he or she is frostbitten.

What to Do

1. Never rub the affected part, and never apply snow to it. Both of these popular "remedies" can only cause further damage to the injured tissues.
2. Rewarm the frostbitten parts rapidly if possible. The best way is to soak them in water at a temperature of 102–105°F. This may take up to 30 minutes, and the victim will feel more and more pain as the tissues thaw.
3. If warm water isn't available, wrap the affected area in blankets.
4. Do *not* use hot water bottles, heating pads, or heat lamps, and don't place the affected part over a stove or a fire—you may cause further damage to tissues.
5. As the tissues thaw, the victim will feel a tingling and burning sensation. The flesh will take on a mottled or purplish color caused by restored circulation.
6. *IMPORTANT:* Once the affected part is thawed, it must not be allowed to refreeze. This will lead to certain amputation.

Heat Stroke

Heat stroke, caused by too much heat, is an emergency. If left in the heat, the victim will die.

The victim will have an oral temperature of 104°F or higher. The skin will be flushed. There will be no sweating, since the victim's body has lost the ability to cool itself by perspiring. The pulse will be strong but rapid. The victim may behave irrationally—or may be unable to move at all. Prompt action is necessary.

What to Do

1. Get the victim to a cool place. An air-conditioned room is best, but failing that, get the victim inside or into the shade.
2. Remove clothing, if possible.
3. Bring the victim's temperature down, but not too far or too fast. At first aim to bring it down to 102°F. Use fans. Sponge or spray the patient with cold water, or place the patient in a tub with cold water—but *no ice.*
4. When the patient's temperature is down to 102°F, stop your cooling efforts for about ten minutes. If, during that period, the temperature rises, resume the cooling treatments. If the temperature continues to fall, cover the patient to prevent shivering; that's the body's way of *raising* the temperature.
5. If the patient is conscious, give fluids—but no stimulants, and nothing hot. If the patient is unconscious, do not give fluids.

Hypothermia

Hypothermia is the opposite of heat stroke: the victim suffers from prolonged exposure to the cold. This does not necessarily mean temperatures below freezing, however. Hypothermia can be caused by temperatures well above 32°F if the person is hungry, wet, overtired, and is overexerting.

Victims of hypothermia will first begin to shiver—the body's mechanism for generating heat. They will then become apathetic, listless, and sleepy. The next stage is unconsciousness, accompanied by very low pulse and respiration. Death will follow if the patient is not treated.

What to Do

1. First, prevent further heat loss. Get the patient to a warm, dry place out of the wind and cold and rain or snow.
2. Rewarm the patient. The best way to do this is to place the patient in a tub of hot water. If this is not possible, use hot water bottles or an electric blanket. Placing the patient close to a source of heat—a fire or radiator—will help. If there is no other source of heat, use your own body heat to warm the patient.

(Note: Simply placing extra covers over the patient will not do the job. He or she does not have enough body heat to warm the space under the covers.)

3. Give the patient hot, sweet liquids.
4. Watch for respiratory or cardiac arrest; be prepared to provide artificial ventilation or CPR.

The victim of hypothermia may look absolutely awful—may even seem dead. Your first reaction may be that any attempt at resuscitation is hopeless. This is not necessarily so. Victims of hypothermia respond well to the proper care and treatment.

Pain

Pain is a message from your body that something is wrong. Any time a person feels prolonged, severe pain, *pay attention. Get medical help.*

Chest pain may be a symptom of angina or heart attack.

Abdominal pain may be a symptom of appendicitis, a ruptured ovary, or any of several other severe medical crises.

Severe head pain unattached to a fall or injury may be a symptom of stroke, or of aneurysm—a ruptured blood vessel—in the brain.

Of course, people may suffer pains in the chest, abdomen, or head that are of no serious consequence whatever. But if the pain is severe and prolonged, you are wise to seek medical help.

Poisoning by Mouth (Ingested)

The first thing to do for a poisoning victim is to call the ambulance. You should assume that what was taken is toxic, and that it was enough to be lethal. What you do next depends upon whether the victim is conscious or unconscious.

What to Do for a Conscious Victim

1. Before you can determine what antidote or treatment to use, you must know what the toxic material was. Locate the container if possible. Manufacturers are required to list any poisonous substances on the label. If you can't find the container, ask the victim what type of substance it was: a household cleaner? a chemical? a medicine?
2. Call Poison Control. (You should list this telephone number in a prominent place along with the numbers of the fire department, police, and ambulance.)
3. Tell Poison Control the patient's age and weight. Tell them what was taken, how long ago, and about how much.
4. Depending upon the substance swallowed, you may be told to dilute the poison by giving the patient a glass of water or milk; or

you may be told to induce vomiting. The only acceptable methods of producing vomiting are placing your finger in the patient's throat, or administering ipecac. Ipecac can be purchased in most drugstore first-aid departments. If you have it on hand, give one tablespoon to children and two tablespoons to adults.

5. If the patient *becomes unconscious,* follow the steps for an unconscious victim, below.

What to Do for an Unconscious Victim

If the victim is unconscious, don't call Poison Control. Poison Control can only tell you how to dilute the poison with fluids or induce vomiting—but *if the patient is unconscious, you mustn't give anything by mouth, and you mustn't induce vomiting.* Instead, call the ambulance and then follow these steps.

1. Place the patient in the *coma* position to prevent aspiration of vomitus in case vomiting occurs.

2. Monitor breathing.

3. Be prepared to offer mouth-to-mouth ventilation and CPR.

Stroke/CVA

A stroke, or cerebrovascular accident, is caused by high blood pressure or by blockage of a blood vessel in the brain. The blockage may be caused by a blood clot, by embolism, or by hemorrhage. Whatever the cause, the result is that circulation to part of the brain is blocked, and that part of the brain is starved for oxygen and fails to function. Frequently, the area of the brain involved dies.

It is important to understand that when brain cells die, the damage is done, and that area of function is lost forever. However, the brain cells in the affected area may not all die. Those that are simply short of oxygen or squeezed by swelling or bleeding may recover. To the degree that the injured areas heal, the patient may recover some brain function. But recovery cannot be complete when portions of the brain have died.

The victim of a minor stroke may or may not lose consciousness. He or she may have a headache, or become dizzy, or suffer a sudden partial loss of memory; may have trouble moving an arm or a leg; or have slurred speech.

If the stroke is more severe, the victim may become paralyzed on one side of the body, and the mouth will be drawn down on that side. He or she may be completely unable to talk, or may slur words. He or she may lose control of bladder and bowels, and may have difficulty breathing. A further indication is that the victim's pupils may be unequal in size—but this does not occur in the conscious patient.

TIA

TIA is an abbreviation for *transient ischemic attack.* (The word *ischemia* refers to lack of blood in a part of the body.) Sometimes called a "little stroke," a TIA is caused by a *temporary* loss of circulation to some portion of the brain. Constriction of an artery in the brain may cause such temporary loss of circulation.

The victim of a TIA may suffer a period of weakness or paralysis or slurred speech lasting from a few seconds to a matter of hours. The most typical attacks last about ten minutes. Between attacks the patient will feel completely normal. A TIA may be a symptom of an impending stroke; such attacks should be taken very seriously.

What to Do

1. Place the victim *on the affected side.* In this way, the airway will be kept open, and the victim will be less likely to aspirate stomach contents if vomiting occurs. Should the victim vomit, sweep it all out of the victim's mouth with your fingers. Be sure the airway is clear.
2. Keep the patient warm; but do not overheat the patient. Use covers.
3. Be sure the patient's airway is kept open; monitor breathing and be ready to assist if breathing stops.
4. Do not give any stimulants. This includes smelling salts.

Unconsciousness (Medical, Without Trauma)

The cause of unconsciousness may or may not be obvious. If it is the result of a fall, for example, the cause is clear; but often there is no immediately identifiable reason for unconsciousness.

What to Do

1. Check the victim's breathing and pulse. If breathing has stopped, begin artificial ventilation. If breathing has stopped and there is no pulse, begin CPR.
2. Place the victim on his or her side. This will minimize the possibility of aspiration of vomit and keep the airway open.

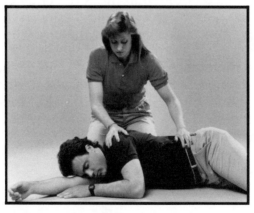

3. Keep the patient warm.
4. Do not try to give an unconscious person anything to eat or drink. The patient has no

control over swallowing and might choke on or aspirate anything you put in his or her mouth.

5. Should the patient vomit, sweep it all out with your fingers. Be sure that the airway is open and clear.

6. Do not move the patient unless there is an immediate danger.

7. Even if the victim recovers consciousness, medical attention is necessary to determine the cause of unconsciousness. A serious condition may underlie the episode.

Symptoms

A final word about symptoms. Every patient will not show all the possible symptoms for a given condition. This does not mean that the condition does not exist. Also, you cannot be sure a condition does exist by the presence of only one symptom. Generally, you should suspect a problem when several of the appropriate symptoms are present in combination. There are of course exceptions. The most important of these is chest pain. Severe chest pain, whether alone or in combination with other symptoms, must be taken as a sign of a heart attack.